UNTIL MY MEMORY FAILS ME

UNTIL MY MEMORY FAILS ME

*Mindfulness Practices for Cultivating
Resilience and Self-Compassion in
the Face of Cognitive Decline*

SHARON LUKERT

Foreword by Elizabeth Mattis Namgyel

SHAMBHALA

Shambhala Publications, Inc.
2129 13th Street
Boulder, Colorado 80302
www.shambhala.com

Cover art: jianjun/stock.adobe.com
Cover and Interior design: Kate E. White

9 8 7 6 5 4 3 2 1

First Edition
Printed in the United States of America

Shambhala Publications makes every effort to print on acid-free, recycled paper.
Shambhala Publications is distributed worldwide by Penguin Random
House, Inc., and its subsidiaries.

Library of Congress Cataloging-in-Publication Data
Names: Lukert, Sharon, author.
Title: Until my memory fails me: mindfulness practices for cultivating resil-
ience and self-compassion in the face of cognitive decline / Sharon Lukert;
Foreword by Elizabeth Mattis Namgyel.
Description: Boulder, Colorado: Shambhala Publications, [2025] | Includes
bibliographical references.
Identifiers: LCCN 2024029038 | ISBN 9781645472971 (trade paperback)
Subjects: LCSH: Memory disorders. | Cognition disorders.
Classification: LCC BF376 .L78 2025 | DDC 153.1/2—dc23/eng/20241119
LC record available at https://lccn.loc.gov/2024029038

The authorized representative in the EU for product safety and
compliance is eucomply OÜ, Pärnu mnt 139b-14, 11317 Tallinn,
Estonia, hello@eucompliancepartner.com.

With love and devotion, this book is dedicated to
ANI PEMA CHÖDRÖN
in gratitude for her steadfast
support, guidance, and kindness to me
through all of life's ups and downs
over these many years.

Contents

List of Practices and Guided Meditations

Foreword

The day before Sharon sent me a request to write the foreword for this book, I stumbled upon a treasure. As I was doing a deep clean in my car, I found a small, crumpled, faded pink sticky note. As fortune would have it, I took the time to see what it was instead of letting the vacuum suck it into the void. My heart stopped when I recognized my mother's familiar handwriting. The fluidity of her script indicated she had written her message at least ten years earlier, after which she contracted familial tremors followed by dementia that required almost five years of 24-7 care.

On this tiny piece of paper, my mother had carefully written a pithy instruction by the seventh-century Buddhist teacher Padmasambhava, who brought Varjayana Buddhism from India to Tibet. She wrote: "Negative circumstances can be transformed into spiritual power and attainment. Make use of this truth. Utilize adversities and obstacles as the path!" I thought, "Such a message should be taken personally!"

I share this with you because over the years I have known Sharon, I have observed her gracefully assimilate her diagnosis and symptoms of mild cognitive impairment (MCI) into her spiritual path and utilize these daunting obstacles as opportunities for growth. True, we don't know what lies ahead, but just as the instructions on that tiny pink piece of paper and in this book encourage us to do, we can make use of our life—even the aspects that we deem "impossible"—because that's when the extraordinary reveals itself to us.

I remember how this looked when caretaking my mother. Although I experienced many challenges watching my mother's slow decline, I tried to never label her situation pathological. We will each have our unique way of engaging our individual circumstances, and I honored whatever my mom had to work out. There were many magical moments. One of my favorites was when, after she could no longer stand up, she requested I take her on a walk. "Bring 'Red' along," she instructed. I had no idea who or what Red was, but I assured her Red would come with. We had many adventures on our virtual walk, never stepping foot outside her room that day.

In the later years, Mom seemed more at peace and yet still fiercely awake. We took care of her life, her body. It was impossible to say what was going on in her mind, although sometimes after not having spoken for many months she would belt out a full sentence, scold us, or say, "Hi, honey!" Most of the time it seemed she had an acute awareness of all the goings on, despite her silence.

In this book, Sharon calls to our attention that we can be at our best when facing hardships and uncertainty. In the beginning of the book, Sharon states her steadfast commitment to growth, "no matter what lies ahead." And in the pages that follow, she generously shares how she honors that commitment. She shares her personal stories, along with the emotional and spiritual tools she uses for coping and thriving, such as meditations and guided contemplations. She underscores the power of open questioning and curiosity. The reader feels supported in their own personal journey.

It's very hands on.

I am delighted that Sharon wrote this book so that we can partake in her wisdom and experience and find solace in the fact that we are never doomed. Even in our darkest hours—even if our memory fails us—when we cultivate an open and adventurous spirit, as Sharon is showing us how to do, we will continue to encounter delightful surprises and experience deep joy.

—ELIZABETH MATTIS NAMGYEL

Acknowledgments

Writing this book has been a cathartic process of coming to terms with my changing body and mind. Without witnessing the courage, humanity, and humor of my dementia ancestors, I would not have had a clue how to handle my recent cognitive decline. This book is as much to honor the life lessons and stories they shared with me as it is to provide some guidance and support for those who, like me, are facing these issues. I first need to acknowledge the inspiration and courage of my dear dementia ancestors. This book would have never been written if I had not known each of them.

My husband, Frank, patiently supported the writing process, reading all my initial attempts and providing honest feedback that ultimately shaped many chapters. He often became the main dishwasher, cook, and house cleaner, allowing me more time to write. While working on this book, we also faced multiple family crises. Our daily walks and conversations have kept our relationship strong through some of the most trying times in the past few years.

Each of my family members has become a part of this book. Although my mother, Lee Wilcox, moved into the latter stages of dementia as I put the finishing touches on the manuscript, she still remembers that I am writing a book and often asks about it. Her love still shines through the fog of lost memory and confusion. The sudden terminal illness of my sister, Janet, was heartbreaking and deeply impacted my writing on a very personal level. My daughter, Allison, encouraged me to keep writing to maintain my cognitive health as well as to bring the book to completion. My son, Kale Williams, is an author himself. He was a mentor, advocate, and guide when this book was just a glimmer of an idea. It has been a gift to watch my young granddaughter, Scarlett, grow and mature. I hope she will be able to read this book years from now and find some solace in hearing my words when I may no longer be able to share my thoughts directly with her.

Elizabeth Mattis Namgyel has been a friend and teacher for several years. She offered spiritual counsel when I was first diagnosed and advice as a fellow writer as I began to construct the book. I am so grateful for her willingness to write the foreword in such a personal and deeply touching way.

I am so grateful to several friends who traveled alongside me, reading and commenting chapter by chapter. Many thanks to Becky Idstrom for your impeccable wordsmithing and Beth Dolder-Zeike for your insightful questions and encouragement. Thanks to Jean Mauss for offering a non-Buddhist perspective and clarifying areas where my sentences were murky. Many thanks to Cathren Murray for being my constant cheerleader and poetry muse. Neil Murray became my technical support and marketing coach, relieving me of the burden of trying to figure out the world of social media on my own.

I had the honor of interviewing two acquaintances who are also living with cognitive changes. They have now become new friends. Sid, as I refer to him in the book, shared his fears, his sense of humor, and his acceptance of every situation as it arose through applying his meditation practice. I was moved by the resilience and courage that Sheri Lowe demonstrates through her ongoing advocacy work with medical students, preparing them for working with people with neurodegenerative disease. By speaking openly about their experiences of living with early cognitive impairment and dementia, they added a fuller perspective of the daily challenges of living with cognitive decline, interfacing with the medical system, and integrating mindfulness into everyday life.

I first met Dr. Nathaniel Chin vicariously through the Dementia Matters podcasts and as the Medical Director of the Alzheimer's Disease Research Center UW–Madison. We became more closely acquainted when we were cospeakers at the Wisconsin Alzheimer's Association Annual Gala in 2023. He later informed me of the elevated amyloid results of the research-based PET scan and then was kind enough to agree to an interview for the book. His passion for educating the public and medical practitioners is contagious. I am deeply grateful for his willingness to share his knowledge and take the time to answer my questions concerning testing, research, medical terminology, and the ever-changing understanding of the physiology of neurodegenerative disease. Thank you for all your work to support those of us in the early and later stages of cognitive decline.

I would be remiss if I did not acknowledge the compassionate care I have received from my medical team. Dr. Gregory Prichett, the retired neuropsychologist from Gundersen Health System in La Crosse, was the first to introduce me to the diagnosis of mild cognitive impairment. His initial guidance, kindness, and referrals set me on the path to discovering so many supportive organizations and people.

This includes Kelsey Flock, the dementia specialist at the La Crosse Aging and Disability Office; CJ Werley, Julie St. Pierre, and Robin McGill (retired) of the Wisconsin Alzheimer's Association; and Bonnie Lee Nuttkinson and Jennifer McAllister from the Alzheimer's Disease Research Center at UW–Madison. I am grateful for the ongoing support, resources, and encouragement each of you has offered me.

One of the advantages of having a published author as a son was that he introduced me to my agent, the incomparable Anna Sproul-Latimer of Neon Literary. Her expertise in coaching me throughout the search for a publisher, contracts, and marketing was invaluable.

The team of editors at Shambhala Publications have been so wonderful to work with. Beth Frankl was immediately interested in the book even in its first rough draft. Jenn Brown has been patient and kind while guiding me through all the steps of publication. Thanks for the expertise of Samantha (Sami) Ripley for all your grammatical corrections and suggestions during the copy-editing phase of production. And a respectful bow to all the staff at Shambhala for believing in the project and bringing *Until My Memory Fails Me* to full fruition.

Nearly everyone involved knew a family member or friend who had Alzheimer's or a related dementia, which made this work so heartfelt and meaningful for everyone. Thank you all, for your commitment and the care you have put into the creation of this book.

UNTIL MY MEMORY FAILS ME

Introduction

Today is a pleasant fall day. It's perfect weather for planting daffodils, as the sky is cloaked in clouds, the breeze soft and warm, and the soil pliable from a recent rain. As I dig into the soil, stuffing each bulb carefully six inches deep, I feel so grateful for this day and my continued ability to garden. Several years ago, I was diagnosed with mild cognitive impairment. Often this diagnosis has treatable causes, but in my case, it is likely due in part to Alzheimer's disease. The diagnosis rocked my world. I wondered how long I would still be able to enjoy the very basic joys of life, such as planting bulbs in the ground. Instead of the anticipated rapid diminishment of my abilities, I have discovered a slow, nuanced process of change. I am realizing there are many moments, days, weeks, months, and years to enjoy a full and rich life while living with cognitive decline, and there are many small simple practices I am incorporating into my days to help me walk that path.

WHAT IS MILD COGNITIVE IMPAIRMENT?

Although I have worked in health care most of my life, I was not familiar with the term *mild cognitive impairment*, or MCI for short. I have known family, friends, and patients who seemed to have a quirky memory, but I thought of this as part of their personality and the normal aging process. I remember my grandmother in the kitchen wearing her blue gingham apron, standing in front of the kitchen counter washed in sunlight. She had flour on her hands and shoes as she held a wooden spoon in the air over the bowl of half-mixed cookie dough. Looking at me intently, she rattled through all the names of her daughters and granddaughters, searching her mind for the right fit for the little girl standing in front of her. I would smile internally at this familiar ritual but wait quietly, holding back the urge to offer up my name, as she found prompting more upsetting than the memory lapse itself. Was this MCI?

With this question in mind, I scoured websites and poured through articles and books, trying to understand what was happening to me and millions of others just like me. I began my search with the Alzheimer's Association website, as my neuropsychologist, Dr. Gregory Prichett suggested. I found their definition for mild cognitive impairment helpful.

Mild cognitive impairment causes cognitive changes that are serious enough to be noticed by the person affected and by family members and friends but do not affect the individual's ability to carry out everyday activities.

MCI can develop for multiple reasons, and individuals living with MCI may go on to develop dementia; others will not. For neurodegenerative diseases, MCI can be an early stage of the disease continuum including for Alzheimer's if the hallmark changes in the brain are present.[1]

I then wondered, What is the difference between normal memory changes and cognitive impairment? This is a difficult but important question to ask if you have any concerns about your memory. The answer is not always definitive or clear-cut, but with the support of a well-trained health professional, it can be determined if the changes you are experiencing are typical for your age or may be suggestive of mild cognitive impairment, which may need further testing. There are different causes for MCI, and many of them are treatable, so it is important to note that not everyone will go on to develop progressive neurodegenerative disease.

To determine if MCI may be caused by Alzheimer's disease (AD) or other neurodegenerative diseases, further exploration is needed. There are two proteins normally in the brain called amyloid and tau. A hallmark change indicating Alzheimer's disease is when these proteins build up abnormally and increase to an elevated level. Amyloid and tau can now be measured through imaging the brain with specialized PET scans and testing spinal fluid. Soon there will likely be a blood test available to detect the elevated presence of amyloid even before there are any cognitive changes. The world of neurocognitive research is on the cusp of major changes to the diagnosis and treatment for early stages of Alzheimer's disease and related dementias.

In my case, MCI is considered likely due to Alzheimer's disease based on two factors: elevated amyloid levels indicated on a PET scan I had as part of a clinical study, and my continued slow decline in cognitive function. For many people like me, it appears that MCI is likely due to Alzheimer's disease.

New breakthroughs in research and clinical trials in recent years offer hope for early, effective treatments in the near future. Research has also proven the positive impact of preventative measures such as exercise, a healthy diet, good sleep, and staying intellectually active. These preventative measures can slow progression before and after a diagnosis of MCI or early dementia. I find hope in the small daily activities I can engage in that may keep my cognitive abilities as strong as possible, for as long as possible. I think of this every time I add a few berries to my yogurt in the morning.

There are at least 5 million Americans who have mild cognitive impairment due to Alzheimer's disease to date.[2] As I found myself standing at this gateway, knowing that dementia will likely be an integral part of my future, I wondered about the other 5 million or so people in this country who are also grappling with similar news. I want those of you who are joining me on this unexpected path to know that you are not alone. This book is for you.

WHY I WROTE THIS BOOK

When I was first diagnosed with mild cognitive impairment, I made a conscious decision to integrate the process of cognitive decline into my lifelong path of spiritual growth and developing an open heart and mind, no matter what lies ahead. I am a passionate, lifelong learner who seeks connection and understanding when faced with adversity. Throughout my life, I have devoted myself professionally and personally to supporting others in developing self-reflection practices, compassion, and loving-kindness. These life lessons are what support me now and what I have to offer to you as a guide through this new unknown territory of changing cognitive abilities. There may not be a medical cure for Alzheimer's disease and related dementias but that does not preclude the ability to meet this illness with dignity, curiosity, and openness.

My ongoing study of Buddhism and psychology, along with my previous experiences as a caregiver, interfaith chaplain, and educator, has placed me in a unique position to reflect upon and write about my lived experience of mild cognitive impairment. Because of my personal struggles with MCI, I want to share what I have learned to provide guidance, assurance, and encouragement to others—life does not end with a neurodegenerative disease diagnosis.

In my work as a chaplain and caregiver I have witnessed the spiritual and emotional challenges that so many confront during major life changes of any kind. I have also witnessed the transformational potential that such challenges can offer. I have worked with people of many faiths and those with no particular belief system, supporting their path toward finding meaning and purpose, no matter their circumstances. In this book, I draw on the emotional and spiritual tools I have learned through my work, many of which are based on Buddhist practices but are accessible to everyone.

The thought of developing Alzheimer's disease can seem like an invasion on your sense of identity and a long-term death sentence. A person with neurocognitive disease may feel doomed to depression, misery, and insurmountable suffering. I have felt overwhelmed by these feelings at times as well, but I refuse to accept that there is no compassion, love, and joy for those living with AD. I have seen for myself when working with the brave folks I've come to think of as my "dementia ancestors" that their humanity would often shine through the thick fog of dementia.

My first acquaintance with Alzheimer's was not a personal one. As a nurse and chaplain, I have walked alongside hundreds of people living with cognitive decline. Once my diagnosis was confirmed, so many faces, names, and stories of those I've cared for and their loved ones came swimming back up into my thoughts. Will I meet memory loss with the same amount of grace as Gabrielle? Remembering Mary's joyful laughter, can I maintain a sense of humor even as I lose my mental functions? What life lessons they taught me over the years will be supportive during the early stages of this progressive and terminal illness? These are some of the topics explored in *Until My Memory Fails Me* with the hope that this will lead each of you into discovering your inner strengths and personal resources to meet this challenge with self-compassion.

HOW TO READ THIS BOOK

We will walk together through the book, with the dementia ancestors and others I have met along this journey, to discover what treasures might be hiding among the weeds and tangles of cognitive decline. To respect the privacy of these subjects, I often use pseudonyms, which are indicated by an asterisk in the text. These life experiences will provide a pathway toward understanding and working with some of the changes that can occur in early stages of Alzheimer's disease and related dementias. Along with sharing these anecdotes and life lessons, I pose open-ended questions throughout the chapters to encourage self-reflection. You will also become acquainted with guided meditations at the end of each chapter that are easily accessible to everyone.

I have processed deep emotions and made sense of my world through poetry since I was a teen. Poetry can describe some of the more visceral aspects of experience that are difficult to put into a narrative form. The poems occasionally shared in *Until My Memory Fails Me* allow a small glimpse into my internal world as I confront the early stages of neuronal tangles and dysfunction.

Most of the practices and meditations are brief and can be done throughout the day—in the grocery store, going for a walk, while doing the dishes. These on-the-spot meditations are simple ways to connect with the present moment and can be a soothing balm, a skillful means to work with challenges now, at this early stage of cognitive change, and develop a positive outlook that can be supportive through the long road of change ahead.

You may already have a formal meditation practice or wish to develop one. The section of meditation instruction will assist you in creating a brief daily practice that allows a time of introspection and a foundation for deepening mindfulness and awareness. Tonglen is a specific form of meditation within the Tibetan Buddhist tradition. My teacher, Pema Chödrön, has called tonglen a particularly beneficial practice for our times as it is a way of increasing compassion for ourselves while also deepening our capacity to show compassion toward and feel connected with all beings.

You are invited to experiment and play with each of these practices to find one—or perhaps a few—that suits your needs best. A meditation that is not interesting to you now may become more relevant at another time.

A thread runs through one chapter to the next, connecting a number of ways to cope and thrive; to find happiness, joy, and love in the midst of changing cognition and decreasing abilities. Just as a garden moves through the seasons with differing blossoms in the spring, summer, and fall, the book moves from encountering the shock and disbelief at the time of diagnosis through working with emotions, stigma, and bias; the process of testing and diagnosis; working with grief and loss; to planning for an unknown future.

While the chapters have a certain continuity from one to the next, each chapter can also stand alone. You may choose to read all or a part of the book at any given time. The book is intended to be an open guide that you can return to now and again when you need further encouragement or your situation has changed.

My ultimate aspiration for this book is that it will inspire a sense of personal meaning and purpose, and encourage each of you who are joining me on this journey to embrace this life-changing disease with as much ease and grace as possible. *Until My Memory Fails Me* can also be a guide to the intimate experience of what it is like to have early cognitive decline. In this way, the book can be of benefit to family and friends of a person living with cognitive changes, and relevant to the many caregivers and health-care providers who become integral team members for those with mild cognitive impairment or early dementia. May this be of benefit for each of you who are joining me at the gateway of early neurocognitive disease.

1

In the Beginning

Shock and the Potential for Transformation

My sister Janet and I were enjoying some outdoor time in my backyard when a friend walked up the drive carrying a batch of morning glories for me. I met him with excitement, my arms wide open, so happy to see these vibrant young plants. I called out, "Oh, the marigolds are here!" My friend stopped in his tracks. He looked at me quizzically, saying "morning glories" in a somber tone.

This could have been an easy slip of the tongue, no different from the frequent faux pas so familiar to folks my age. But the word *marigold* became stuck in my brain, like a skipping record. When I was pointing out the various vegetables I planted in our raised bed, I called each one a marigold. The tomatoes, lettuce, carrots—no matter what I was trying to describe, "marigolds" came out of my mouth. I didn't seem to be able to correct myself, which baffled and frustrated me. Janet giggled. I'm not sure if it was a nervous laugh or she really thought this was funny. I didn't.

This was when I became suspicious about my symptoms. It was early June of 2021 and a beautiful summer day along the Upper Mississippi River in La Crosse, Wisconsin, which borders both Iowa and Minnesota. Like the rest of the country, my husband, Frank, and I were enjoying a respite from the pandemic—a brief window of time between becoming fully vaccinated and the onslaught of the Delta variant yet to come later in the summer. Family gatherings were a welcome distraction from the isolation and pandemic fear that permeated our lives for the past year.

I had retired from working in the Spiritual Care Department at Gundersen Health System Hospital, just as the pandemic was ramping up, after nearly ten years in the department and a total of twenty years in chaplaincy. I missed my work as a chaplain and an educator but was relieved to be off the front lines of the COVID crisis. This did not spare me from the virus, however. In November of 2020, I contracted a mild case of COVID-19. I recovered from the acute phase, but a chronic cough has now lingered for years.

Finally we could visit my mom in person again and take her on an outing from the assisted living facility that she called home. For a year I had visited her through the window, speaking by phone, through the bitter cold, snow, and rain. It was so comforting to be in the same room with her again even while keeping a distance and wearing masks. That spring, Frank and I also traveled to visit my son, Kale, and his wife, Rebecca, in Portland, Oregon. In late May my daughter, Allison, her husband, Steven, and my then three-year-old granddaughter, Scarlett, drove from Phoenix, Arizona, to visit us. Then in June, Janet was visiting for a week as she was making plans to retire to this area from Colorado with her husband, Joe, the following year.

This was more social activity than I had had in a long time. It was refreshing, and like much of the nation, we were breathing a sigh of relief, believing the worst of the pandemic was behind us. The mood was elated and festive as we reunited with family and were hopeful that the pandemic was coming to a close. This was also the time when I became aware of some concerning cognitive changes.

I am generally very organized, and I pride myself on being prompt. And yet I had missed more than six appointments within as many weeks. Frank assured me this was normal aging memory loss, but it did not feel normal to me.

The tipping point came during Janet's visit. We were spending a lot of time together as I became her quasi-tour guide as she explored housing options in the area. As I was driving around the local streets and neighborhoods, it took a lot of concentration for me to keep up with the conversation and find my way at the same time. I found this very tiring but brushed it off as just a part of being so active again after such a long time of isolation.

Then there was the "marigold moment." Later in the same week, Janet missed an important appointment because I had mistaken the date. My heart sank when I realized that I had mixed up the days and had even written it incorrectly on my calendar. I was now convinced something beyond normal aging was happening. The next day I called for an appointment with the neuropsychologist I had seen previously.

TESTING AND DIAGNOSIS

Two years earlier I had some concerns about my cognitive abilities. There was that time when I did not recognize a colleague I work with daily in the hallway at the hospital. On another occasion, Frank and I were at a car lot as we were considering buying a new car. It was on a centrally located street corner in downtown La Crosse, yet I couldn't place where we were. I mentioned these and a few other instances to my primary care physician, who ordered a series of neurological tests in the summer of 2019.

At that time, the neuropsychologist, Dr. Prichett, said the test results were in the normal range, except for one or two areas that were a bit lower than the rest. We discussed the test results and he inquired about my stress level. My job was demanding intellectually, physically, and emotionally as I was responsible for tending to the spiritual needs of patients in the hospital and overseeing all aspects of the Clinical Pastoral Education program, including the full admissions process, creating the curriculum, facilitating classes, and working individually with students and staff. Dr. Prichett suggested the low areas in the testing scores were probably related to this stress rather than any significant cognitive changes. He recommended I cut down on my stress level any way that I could, even suggesting I consider retiring sooner rather than later. He was fairly confident once I retired and my stress decreased, these issues would resolve on their own. However, he also offered follow-up testing if I felt it was warranted in the future. Given this information, I prepared to retire in the summer of 2020. Then the pandemic hit. As it was becoming full blown in the early spring, life inside the walls of the hospital was becoming chaotic. The hospital was full of very ill patients, and all departments were asked to decrease expenses as routine care and surgeries were cut back to a minimum. I was finding it more difficult to keep up with the daily changes in protocol and massive decisions that needed to be made and implemented quickly. Given that the Spiritual Care Department needed to cut expenses, I opted to retire earlier than planned, assisting both the department in curbing expenses and relieving myself of the added stress.

So, in the summer of 2021, Frank and I sat in the office with Dr. Prichett once again after another two-hour round of testing. His tone was more somber this time. He told us the tests showed a significant decline in several areas, specifically in my ability to pay attention and in my processing time, from the previous tests in 2019. He gave me a diagnosis of mild cognitive impairment (MCI). At the time, I didn't really know what this meant. He told us a statistic as to how many people with MCI go on to develop Alzheimer's disease (AD), but I was in too much shock to really take it in at the time. He also gave us a handout about MCI and suggested we look at the Alzheimer's Association website and familiarize ourselves with the early signs of Alzheimer's. He said that I was at an increased risk for developing Alzheimer's disease within the next one to five years. He now wanted to see me back every six months to see if my symptoms were progressing. We were stunned.

RUPTURE

Having lived six decades, I am no stranger to crisis points in my life. Like most people who have lived long enough to have a past, I organize my memories according to what happened before and after certain incidents. Before and after the birth of a child. Before and after the death of a loved one. And then there are the societal before-and-afters. The death of Martin Luther King Jr., Hurricane Katrina, and now the pandemic.

The day I was diagnosed with MCI became one more personal time marker for me: another life-changing event that shifted my reality.

As a nurse and even more so in my twenty years as a chaplain, I was often called on to support patients and their families through loss and times of despair. These seminal situations would later become a marker of time within their lives. The actual crisis can be a crushing blow, leaving the people who are impacted with an uprooted sense of reality. How they relate to the world and their sense of self have often been completely disrupted. Life goes on, and yet they have been deeply changed. When someone going through such an occurrence can embrace this tearing of the fabric of their lives—if they can stay with the chaotic, often numbing thoughts and feelings—transformation can happen at a deep and lasting level.

I remember Anna*, a hospice patient who was young—in her fifties—when she was diagnosed with advanced and metastasized colon cancer. Her situation was dire, and she only had a few months left to live. She had no family to turn to and didn't know what to do as she now needed round-the-clock care. Anna wanted to release herself from the physical pain of dying and to protect her friends from the emotional pain of caring for her. She began to contemplate suicide. I remember meeting with her one evening in the hospital when she asked me to acquire some drugs for her so she could end her life. I sat beside her as the sun set outside her hospital window and listened to her despair and fear of what lay ahead for her final months. She was in a desperate situation, there was no denying it. This sudden, unexpected diagnosis with no possible treatment and little time left—her options were limited.

I did not try to talk her out of her feelings and desire to escape. Silently I sat with her for a long time before I spoke, not knowing what comfort I could offer. When I did speak, my words were tenuous and soft. "I wonder, what's ahead for you? None of us know what the future holds. Even when the doctors have given you such dire news, I'm curious what might happen next. Your situation seems so solid and certain, but I am curious, what other possibilities might arise? What gifts may be waiting for you in this process?" This stopped her, and I could see from the look on her face that she was surprised I wasn't taking a side, either assisting her or trying to talk her out of her despair. Her expression softened, and I could see that she was beginning to break through the frozen state of fear. Our visit ended quickly after that and I left, unsure of how supportive I had been or what she would choose to do.

Later that week, to her surprise, her friends stepped forward to support her. Anna found herself in a friend's loving home when she was released from the hospital, with all the care she needed and a beautiful view from her hospital bed. I was honored to be her chaplain and to witness this transformation unfolding for her. Anna faced her situation head-on. Once the initial crisis was met, she used her illness as an opportunity to make peace with past grievances and to strengthen her sense of God's presence. Even as she lay in her hospital bed, unable to eat or drink anymore, she marveled at the birds outside her window and the warm sun on her face. She looked forward with curiosity to what she might encounter in the unknown reaches after death. Anna died with a warm and open heart, embracing life and death as it was. In her case, she decided to embrace the unknown and the uncertainty of her precarious situation.

Anna's story is one of many, many personal stories of transformation I was honored to witness as a chaplain. The way so many people have shared their lives—and their deaths—with me has influenced my own responses when encountering crisis. I have learned to value and embrace impermanence and uncertainty as a gift rather than something to fear. This is a shift that is not easy but can change our perspective when unwanted circumstances intrude upon us, like a diagnosis of neurodegenerative disease.

Now I am being called upon to embrace the unknown future for myself. My words to Anna come back to me as a reminder to not shut down the possibilities ahead just because of a medical diagnosis. It is not a life sentence as much as a glimpse of one aspect of the road ahead. It is just one piece of a map, not the whole map and certainly not the territory itself.

BUDDHISM AND THE BARDO

I have practiced Tibetan Buddhism for more than thirty years, and I had the good fortune to meet Pema Chödrön in the early 1990s at the Berkeley Shambhala Center. Pema, a Tibetan Buddhist monastic who is well known as a teacher and an author, often visited the Bay Area in California, which was once her home. I met her when she was leading a weekend meditation retreat and felt an immediate connection to her and her teachings about compassion. That weekend I took refuge, which is similar to being baptized in Christianity, and became one of Pema's students. Tibetan Buddhism and Pema's teachings have had a deep and profound effect on how I approach life, especially when difficulties arise. At that time, I was full of self-loathing. The idea of being kind and compassionate toward myself, as well as others, was a welcome and soothing balm. Tibetan Buddhism echoed much of my own experiences and beliefs, and finding a community of practitioners provided me with a wider context and new ways of working with emotions and life challenges, including times of crisis.

The bardo is one of the concepts in Tibetan Buddhism that resonates for me. *Bardo* is a Tibetan term that in its most basic translation means "transition" or "intermediate stage." There is the bardo of life, between birth and death; the bardo after death; and another bardo of transitioning from life to death. The idea of a bardo can also be applied to all the small transitions of daily life. These bardos may be small but easy to recognize once one begins paying attention to them. A goodbye kiss in the morning as you leave the house, entering a building, closing a door behind you—all these are the small daily transitions we barely notice. This is the view of bardo I have found most supportive in my own life, in my work as a chaplain, and especially now as I cope with the changes of mild cognitive impairment. If we can become aware of and comfortable with the daily bardos, it can help us prepare for the larger transitions, such as a personal crisis, a new diagnosis, and even death.

As a chaplain, I learned to look for these daily times of transition and to consider them as potential moments for openness, each a small death and rebirth. Recognizing these small moments of change provides a fresh start to whatever may happen next. In the hospital, standing outside a patient's room, I would prepare to enter another unique situation. As I paused and slowly applied antiseptic gel to my hands, I would take a deep breath in and out, letting go of what had occupied my mind just moments ago. I would feel refreshed, with an open heart and a clear mind, before entering another person's world, as yet unknown to me.

PAUSE PRACTICE

Pema teaches a practice she calls the "Pause Practice" to help us pay attention to the many shifts we experience throughout the day. The instructions are to intentionally pause during your day, especially when you are feeling a strong emotion, and notice what you are feeling, the angle of the sunlight in the room, a sound. The practice is to pause, take a few deep breaths, and allow yourself to feel what you are feeling, be aware of your surroundings, and then let it go and move on. This is what I would do outside a patient's room before entering or in the middle of a crisis situation where I would be called on to support the family. I would teach my chaplain students this technique so they would have a tool to work with the multitude of emotions they would encounter through their service to others in the hospital.

Some transitions are more difficult and life-changing than others. These are times when the idea of a bardo is more evident and can even feel quite harsh. Another Buddhist teacher, Pema Khandro Rinpoche, writes about bardo as a rupture, describing the experience of grief after the death of a loved one. She writes, "We are not given options, there is no room for negotiation, and the situation cannot be rationalized away or covered up by pretense. There is a total rupture in our who-I-am-ness, and we are forced to undergo a great and difficult transformation."[3]

Hearing the diagnosis of mild cognitive impairment ruptured our world and began a new paradigm shift into a reality where my cognitive abilities are on the decline. In that moment, after leaving the doctor's office, I don't think either Frank or I could even begin to truly process the life-altering transition born through those hours of testing and hearing the results. Walking out of the clinic, the sky was bright blue, and it was a warm and sunny day. Just like the shifted reality of someone who has just lost a loved one, the world somehow seemed unreal and yet uniquely vivid. Both, at once. We needed time and activity to help us wrap our heads around what all these new terms and medical jargon meant to our lives. So, of course, as we often do, we went for a walk.

The bardo teachings go on to assure the meditator that over time, and as we become more familiar and comfortable with these transitions, we can learn to relax when there is sudden change. Entering this new bardo of cognitive decline, I learned firsthand that this takes time. It can't be rushed. I needed to find my own way with this new sense of groundlessness. The Pause Practice became a sort of lifeline for me at that time. This was one of the important early lessons for me—to allow myself to find my own rhythm, one pause, one breath at a time. For anyone facing this same type of major life transition, I hope you can find the internal gentleness and patience to allow yourself to turn toward this new reality slowly, bit by bit, in your own way and at your own pace.

STAY IN THE PRESENT MOMENT?!

When I was given the diagnosis of mild cognitive impairment, my doctor advised me to stay in the present moment. This seemed odd and a bit of an overused cliché to my Buddhist ears. He followed up on this advice by explaining that some people obsess about the diagnosis, making their lives miserable, often thinking everything they experience is related to MCI. However, at the same time, he also advised me to educate myself on the early signs of Alzheimer's disease. He told me I am at a high risk of developing Alzheimer's within the next one to five years.

This became a paradox I've been leaning into: how to find a balance between not overly obsessing about the diagnosis and, at the same time, taking appropriate action to educate myself and make helpful lifestyle changes.

In retrospect, this has taken a while to bring into balance, and this balance is constantly shifting. At first I tried to make sense of this new terrain of cognitive decline. I relied on some of my tried-and-true managerial skills from my working days. I held several administrative positions over the years as an office manager; home health aide coordinator; director of Gampo Abbey, a monastic monastery in Nova Scotia; and most recently as the program manager of the Clinical Pastoral Education program training chaplain residents at Gundersen Health System. In my final position, I managed educational programs, wrote theoretical papers, and met with student chaplains to assist them in their pastoral development and practice of chaplaincy. I began applying these well-honed administrative and learning skills to my cognitive challenges. I told myself I was attempting to manage my cognitive challenges, but without realizing it, I was trying to control something that could not be controlled: my own mental decline.

I created a chart comparing what I perceived as my mental gifts and challenges. I tried to link them together so my gifts could compensate for the difficulties of my challenges—a sort of checks and balances, like you might try when balancing a checkbook. I created a complex weekly schedule to cut down on missed appointments. I created pages of checklists for tasks and things to do. All to avert and delay any further signs of my depleted cognitive abilities. I created mind maps as a creative way to ponder the many existential questions swimming through my thoughts. These were posted around my desk.

If you ask my husband, and if he were being honest, I think he would tell you I had drifted into an obsessive mode of coping. After months of these strategies, which failed to slow down the changes I was noticing, I realized I was trying to manage away the diagnosis. It's a similar approach I had used before regarding weight gain and food issues. Often, in the past with these minor concerns, it would work. But how do you "manage" the deterioration of your cognitive skills? How does organizing heal the ailing neurons and protein buildup in the brain? It's like trying to erase cancer from the body by doing push-ups. The wrong medicine for the ailment.

Another pitfall I waded deeply into in those first few months was a form of hypervigilance. If you have never experienced hypervigilance, it is a heightened state of arousal, stress, or sensitivity to certain stimuli. Imagine being in a dark alley with a stranger walking toward you holding something long, straight, and shiny in one hand. Is your pulse racing? Having this sense of heightened awareness in everyday life, when there isn't an imminent threat, is the experience of hypervigilance.

As a survivor of abuse, I am keenly aware of this state of intensified sensitivity. It did not surprise me when I began worrying about my memory quickly deteriorating with every slip of a word or pause to remember what was on the grocery list. I can see why the doctor warned me about this, and I can understand why anyone who is newly diagnosed would respond this way. I had no reference point for distinguishing between a "normal" slip and a sign of further decline.

Where was the yardstick? This is a question that still haunts me today and one that we will revisit throughout this book.

Hypervigilance is a pathological way of looking at this phenomenon of being hypersensitive to certain circumstances. From a Buddhist perspective, heightening our sense of awareness in general is a positive by-product of meditation. From my perspective, mindful awareness can shift into hypervigilance when the awareness has a particular laser-beam focus that is critical or fearful or has a negative focus. That sharp focus can distort the magnitude of the situation and any shadow or bump in the night can be perceived as a threat.

My meditation practice has allowed me to relax the tightness of that laser-beam focus, recognizing these troubling situations for what they are: distortions of my perception caused by hypervigilance. This tight gaze is constantly looking for what is going wrong. I use meditation to relax this overzealous alertness in two ways. During formal meditation, as I sit on the cushion, focusing on my breath, my mind softens and I allow these thoughts to come and go without holding on to them. This allows a break in the obsessive mind, even if it is only for a breath or two. This gap, a tiny bardo, allows me to see there is little substance to what I am trying to make solid.

Another way I use my meditation to relax this obsessive tendency is in the moment—on the spot, such as when I am standing in the grocery store mentally chastising myself because I forgot what I was supposed to pick up for dinner. The information just isn't anywhere in my brain. I'm feeling frustrated and angry with myself. In that moment, if I can recognize what I am doing and stop to pause and take a deep breath, I can see how I am creating my own pain. When I breathe out, I can remember to let go of those feelings with gentleness and loving-kindness toward myself. Then I can relax and carry on with the rest of the shopping, even if it means I go home without the milk and eggs.

It took me a few months to find balance between hypervigilance on one end and simply noticing on the other. I don't want to oversimplify this process, as it is still emotionally painful as new symptoms arise. But when I can at least accept with a little grace that forgetfulness is a new part of who I am, then I can still be happy and kind to myself and others, even when I may not get things done or remember things as well as I believe I used to.

I realize now Dr. Prichett was not referring to the metaphysical meaning of time when he suggested I stay in the present moment. Each moment is continually changing into the next, so we can't really stay there. We can only stay with our experience as it unfolds from one moment to the next. My sense of staying in the present moment in this sense has expanded to include feeling the intense emotions of confusion and overwhelm. It is not the static bliss this cliché might imply but rather a dynamic mix of being with whatever arises and meeting it in the best way I can in the moment. This isn't always the way I would like to meet these moments, but it's the best I can do at the time.

By developing loving-kindness toward oneself, along with patience and a good dose of humor, meeting the daily challenges can soften into moments of acceptance and tenderness. Using the tools of self-reflection or the Pause Practice provides a foundation to discover and enhance self-love based on our humanness and an intimate understanding of the many different aspects that make us who we are, including our foibles, failures, and triumphs.

GUIDED MEDITATION

Pause Practice

The Pause Practice is an excellent tool for working with change on a day-to-day basis as well as with the major shifts in our lives born through crisis and loss. There are several versions of this practice. I have taught this practice to both patients and students, as it is easy to learn and can be applied immediately in any situation. This is also a practice that can be used whether you have a formal meditation practice or not.

To begin, it is best to try to use this practice a few times each day. It might be helpful to post reminders at first, such as on the bathroom mirror, so you can pause just after brushing your teeth. Coupling the practice with daily routines will help you establish it as a new habit. Becoming familiar with it in this way makes it easier to bring it to mind when you have strong feelings or are facing a challenge. You can do this practice anywhere, anytime, alone or on a crowded bus. You can be standing, sitting, or lying down.

To begin, take a slow deep breath in, hold it for a few seconds, and slowly let it out.

While you do this a few times—three breaths are generally recommended—notice how you feel. You may notice any of the following or none at all. It doesn't matter what you notice; there is no right or wrong.

* Physically—any tension, heart racing, warm or cold hands
* Mentally—clearheaded, tired, dull, distracted
* Emotionally—happy, sad, excited, angry

Whatever you feel physically, mentally, and emotionally, allow it to just be. There is no need to change it or judge it. In this way, you are touching in with the natural flow of your energy. Energy moves and changes all on its own. There is no need to do anything but notice.

With the last breath, breathe out deeply, look up and out, let go of attending to your feelings, let go of the practice itself, and carry on with your activities.

This is a very simple and yet profound way to pay attention to what you are feeling while developing the habit of letting those feelings be without judgment, resistance, or tightly holding on to them. Without processing your emotions or pushing them away, you can simply witness what you are experiencing without becoming overwhelmed or swept away by them. You can become more aware of the subtle shifts and the small bardos of transition that are happening all the time throughout the day—from one breath to the next, a small death and rebirth.

2

Dancing with Cognitive Decline

Everything relies on everything else in the cosmos in order to manifest—whether a star, a cloud, a tree, or you and me.

—THICH NHAT HANH, *The Art of Living: Peace and Freedom in the Here and Now*

The Vietnamese Zen Buddhist teacher Thich Nhat Hanh coined the term *interbeing* to describe how all aspects of life are intimately connected and dependent on one another. Consider how a garden grows. It takes a combination of soil, water, sunlight, seeds, and attention to grow a flourishing garden of vegetables and flowers. It is this type of interdependence, or interbeing, that Thich Nhat Hanh refers to when he says, "Everything relies on everything else in the cosmos in order to manifest." This is true physically, as it is the interbeing—the interconnection—of our cells, tissue, blood, hormones, neurons, and consciousness that composes our living body. Even how our neurons relate to each other is an expression of the interconnectedness that creates our unique sense of self. Interbeing extends out into our family units, society, oceans and deserts, and as far reaching as the infinite universe. At every level of existence, we "inter-are," as Thich Nhat Hanh would say.

We are all relational beings. Emotionally, intellectually, and spiritually, we grow, learn, and heal in relationship internally and with one another. Love, attention, conflict, and repair take place between and with one another. This is the dance of interbeing we engage in with everyone in our lives. When I was diagnosed with mild cognitive impairment, my life changed. Life also changed for my husband and family. This is true for each person living with this disease; the people they are connected to are also affected. I am fortunate and privileged to have a close, loving, and supportive partner. Some people face this illness alone, without this type of support. Others refuse support offered by loved ones and friends as they are unaware of their cognitive changes or out of an attempt to preserve their independence and identity. A diagnosis of neurocognitive disease impacts every level of our relationships as the rupture to our sense of well-being is deep and our expectations now and for the future shift. It is as if the tempo of the music has changed so the usual movements don't quite match up anymore. Learning to dance with this new chapter in life takes patience, tenderness, and compassion for yourself and others.

From the moment Frank and I stepped into Dr. Prichett's office, we began this new dance together. Before the appointment began or the neurological testing was completed, Frank was handed a questionnaire to fill out. He was asked if I could dress myself and take my medications independently, and how much assistance he provided for me daily. These seemed extreme at the time, as I still functioned independently. The form went on, inquiring about how he was handling his role as a caregiver. Up until this point, we were not in the designated roles of patient and caregiver. Before the diagnosis was even confirmed, as he checked off the boxes that told only a small piece of the story of our changing relationship, Frank had acquired this new title of caregiver and the presumed responsibilities that go along with it.

THE JAR OF PASTA SAUCE

In this new dance, we occasionally miss a beat or bump into each other. There have been times when Frank seemed to take over, assuming I was not capable of a task I can still do well. One such moment led to tears, fear, and accusations over a misplaced jar of pasta sauce. Like a *Where's Waldo?* book, the jar was missing in action but really hiding in plain sight. Before we actually found the jar, Frank was certain it was another sign of my decline, as I had already lost a number of items. Even though my track record for losing items included two pairs of eyeglasses and a cutting board, I was certain I had not misplaced the jar of sauce. I felt prejudged and misunderstood.

It was a hard night as I began to doubt my ability to gauge my cognitive abilities. Maintaining awareness of my weaknesses and continued strengths provides some sense of control. Bringing this into doubt was terrifying for me. If I was losing awareness of my cognitive skills this soon, my decline was accelerating at a faster pace than I was prepared for. I cried, Frank consoled me, and we went to bed. The next day, I found the jar in question where it belonged in the kitchen cabinet, hiding behind a ketchup bottle on the top shelf. A few days later, Frank and I were able to sit down and talk about this incident in a calm, honest, and gentler manner than we could in the heat of the moment.

We have come to rely on this new choreography for moving through misunderstandings and conflict toward repair and connection. There are times when I feel too overwhelmed, distracted, or exhausted to talk about what is bothering me. And there are times when Frank has not been ready for the deeper conversations about the future that I am anxious to address while I still can. But we have found a way of sharing our need to talk, even if we are not prepared to talk about it in the moment. We can then circle back in a do-si-do fashion to the topic at a time when we are both ready to plunge into the conversation.

THE EIGHTFOLD PATH

The Buddha offered the Noble Eightfold Path for his students to follow to guide them toward inner peace and liberation. The eight steps of this path are right view, right intention, right speech, right conduct, right livelihood, right effort, right mindfulness, and right understanding. These steps are not linear but are intricately related, and as a practice, they function together. Using the word *right* in this context does not imply a binary of right or wrong but in essence means whole or wholesome. Just as it takes many elements for a tomato to ripen, all of the steps on the eightfold path create a full and whole guide toward awakening. The eightfold path continues to be a central principle and guide for students of Buddhism today.

The third step of the path, right speech, invites you to consider the power of communication. What we say and what we hear from others has a strong influence on our worldview, what we think, how we feel, and how we behave. I find that working with the concept of right speech is one of the most difficult and yet rewarding elements of the eightfold path. It is hard to do, but you can begin to see results relatively quickly as this practice has the potential to affect our relationships as well as our mindset.

SELF-REFLECTION

Much like a garden hoe and trowel are essential for cultivating a garden, self-reflection is a foundational tool for working with right speech. By cultivating the ability to contemplate and review what we have said or how we have responded to what was said to us in order to grow and understand ourselves better, we can begin to see patterns and take small steps to try something new. Through reflecting on our interactions and how they have impacted ourselves and others, we can begin to weed out patterns that may be causing anger, denigration, or hurt feelings and cultivate more loving-kindness for ourselves and others.

The type of self-reflection I am referring to is different from rumination or repetitive, negative thoughts, which can be debilitating and detrimental to a person's mental health. Self-reflection in this context is a form of practice and personal inquiry with a gentle and loving touch.

There are several routines one can adopt that support self-reflection. You may already employ one of these in your daily life. The simple act of thinking about something you said is a form of reflection that you can build on and support by either writing down your thoughts, talking to someone about it, or reviewing your conversations at the end of the day. Noting what interactions you felt good about and what ones left you with negative feelings can help you to cull out the weeds in your communication. Over time, certain patterns may become more obvious, and you can develop more awareness in the moment of what speech is beneficial and nourishing.

Applying self-reflection to daily communication takes patience and compassion for yourself and others. It is a slow dance, but one where real understanding and change can happen internally as you become more familiar with the workings of your own mind, and externally as you begin to understand what drives the other person's point of view. During the missing-jar incident, I was feeling anxious and worried about my potentially accelerating symptoms. Frank was tired at the time and feeling frustrated with what he perceived as my lack of awareness and memory loss in that moment. Realizing and accepting these differing perspectives when we talked about our feelings later helped us move through the conflict and repair the misunderstanding, which strengthened our relationship. Whether you practice self-reflection alone or in partnership with a loved one, it can become an indispensable tool when facing any type of conflict or crisis.

ADJUSTMENT

Adjusting to this new way of moving together seems to happen in small, nuanced shifts within day-to-day living. At first Frank seemed less aware of my changing cognitive abilities than I was. Often when I would mention something I had forgotten, he would chalk it up to normal forgetfulness that comes with aging. In all honesty, I do seem to have a better short-term memory than he does at times. But my symptoms are in other cognitive areas as well. I have many blanks when it comes to who people are and events that happened last year or a month ago. Also, keeping track of time and schedules is perplexing to me now. Yet I can help Frank find the keys or remember what we watched on TV last night. And I found the jar of pasta sauce. This decline is quirky, so I can see why it would not be obvious to him at times. Lately I rely on Frank more for a reality check. When I notice a new change, I tend to report it to him. If the change becomes a new pattern, he can help me recognize it. This has also helped him to tune in to the strangeness of these changes. More recently, he has begun to notice some changes that I have not, such as times I have forgotten to turn off the stove. By sharing our observations with each other, we can stay more in step with these shifts as they are happening. Then we can talk about and decide together how to address any issues as they arise.

As a chaplain, I have witnessed many different kinds of relationships, and each couple, family, and group of friends has their own style of communicating and unspoken rules that govern what is and is not said. Often these rules have not been scrutinized through the lens of right speech or self-reflection. Because of well-established patterns of communicating, I have seen many people struggle with how to share difficult news or discuss openly their feelings with one another when they are in the midst of a crisis. These patterns are not always helpful or honest. The good news is that these unspoken rules and patterns can change, as our way of communicating is interdependent and fluid. Patiently you can begin to apply self-reflection as you are able in your own life, with gentleness, loving care, and the lightness of humor for all the missteps that are inevitable along the way. Paying attention and practicing new ways of speaking with each other can then support more open dialogue when emotions are running high and there is a difficult situation at hand. This is one way to develop a deeper awareness of how we "inter-are."

COMMUNICATION AND COGNITIVE IMPAIRMENT

For someone whose communication may be impaired due to cognitive issues, self-reflection can be a way to sustain a sense of agency and patience with yourself and others as long as you can. Verbal communication is one of the challenges for many people with MCI and other neurocognitive disorders. Much of this is a result of damage to certain areas in the brain that allow speech, memory, and logical thinking, which are out of a person's control. When it is difficult for someone to express themselves, it can be unclear if the person is unwilling to talk about what is happening to them, unaware of these changes, or unable to express their experience. I am at the very early stages of this process, yet I have had more trouble mixing up words, such as the marigold/morning glory debacle, and I often forget what Frank has previously told me, so my questions become repetitive. There are times, especially when I am feeling overwhelmed, when my thoughts are too jumbled to get them out of my mouth. This can be frustrating for me and for the listener. I have learned to slow down and take a breath when this happens, but sometimes I just let it go, realizing that what I was trying to say was not worth the effort it was taking to say it.

LOSS OF INSIGHT OR DENIAL?

In hospice, many years ago, I worked with David*, a gentleman in his late sixties with Lewy body dementia, and his wife, Dorothy*. He was in the latter stages of the disease and living in a skilled nursing facility at the time I met them. Most of my visits were with Dorothy, who was grieving an untimely and prolonged end to their relationship. One of the most frustrating aspects of the disease process for Dorothy was that David had no awareness of his decline and all the changes that his illness dictated. This created tension and conflict in their marriage. Dorothy confided in me with tears in her eyes that her greatest regret was they were never able to talk about and face this illness together, because David lacked awareness of the changes in himself. They were unable to face this in partnership, the way they had met so many other challenges throughout their many years together. This lack of insight into declining abilities can be one of the losses imposed by neuro-degenerative disease and can stimy open, mutual collaboration with loved ones.

Seeking ways to enhance our communication skills as a couple during this early juncture in my own process provides Frank and me with a way to begin this journey with as much grace, humor, and understanding as we can muster. With self-reflection as a tool, open and caring communication is the garden we are cultivating together. We hope this will allow us a strong foundation for a long time to come. But my eyes are wide open to the fact that my communication skills, as well as my awareness and insight regarding my decline, may not remain intact. My symptoms may interfere with my ability to engage in complex verbal exchanges in the future. Knowing this instills a strong motivation to pay attention now to what I say and how I say it. As one hospice coworker used to say, the most important thing is to stay current in relationships. Say what you intend to say now, as no one is promised a tomorrow.

HARRY AND GABRIELLE

I knew one couple years ago who danced together gracefully with cognitive decline, even when the person with Alzheimer's disease was no longer able to be a mutual partner. Harry and Gabrielle were devoted to each other and the life they had built together living near Gampo Abbey, a Western Buddhist monastery on Cape Breton Island in Nova Scotia, Canada. Harry was a tall, thin man with bushy gray hair that always seemed a bit disheveled. He was a quiet, intellectual type, with a warm smile and a twinkle of curiosity in his eyes. He was an accomplished carpenter and a strong conservationist, tending to the forest that surrounded their land. Gabrielle was outgoing and warm, with a slight build and graying hair; her eyes sparkled too with a love for life and engaging conversation. I had known Harry and Gabrielle since 1993 through the many years I visited and lived at Gampo Abbey.

They came daily to Gampo Abbey to share the noon meal with the residents. This was a social time, as we broke the morning silence of meditation and study. Harry enjoyed the company of the men in the facilities department. They discussed the care of the forest on the property, how much wood to put up for the coming winter, and how to fix the unending repairs required of the old structure of the main building. Gabrielle would listen to the stories of the young people who moved in and out of the Abbey. Her laughter could be heard across the dining room. They were an integral part of the Gampo Abbey community for more than twenty years, as senior practitioners, meditation instructors, and participants in the daily life alongside the residents, guests, and staff.

In 2006, when I was the director of Gampo Abbey, Harry and I sat together on their porch surrounded by the sweet smell of summer pine, talking about their changing needs as they aged. It was becoming clear that Gabrielle was going through some cognitive changes, and Harry was looking frail and weary. He sought out my counsel as he knew of my background in caregiving and health care. Outside their home on some old wooden chairs, grayed with age, listening to the stream babbling down in the crevasse below, we talked about possible plans for the two of them, while Gabrielle napped.

When I had first arrived for this visit, Gabrielle was busily cooking in the kitchen. I watched as Harry gently redirected her when she became distracted. Quietly he would shut off the burners when she walked away from the stove. He followed her around, taking the milk carton out of the oven, placing it back in the fridge where it belonged without correcting her but keeping her safe. It was an exhausting dance for Harry and an unconscious one for her.

Gabrielle seemed as content as ever and appeared unaware of the changes to her memory and ability to function on a day-to-day level.

I marveled at their relationship. They were working with these major life changes of aging bodies and deteriorating brain cells with grace. But this dance was draining for Harry. I worried about his ability to keep up the level of vigilance I witnessed earlier in their kitchen.

As Harry and I talked, I sipped my tea slowly, taking my time to consider the options and what might work in their very particular situation. The closest town was an hour drive over a mountain. Would Gabrielle accept outside help? Would Harry be comfortable with strangers in their home? How could our small community at Gampo Abbey support them? These questions lingered in my mind before

I was ready to voice them. I was familiar with a model of care called Share the Care (see Resources on p. 191) that guides friends through arranging a care team, but how could this work in our remote setting on the cliffs of Cape Breton Island?

I began to think out loud with Harry about their changing needs, watching his expression, trying to gauge his thoughts and concerns. After a long conversation, Harry laid out his desire for help with Gabrielle, but she is wary of strangers. He did not want someone else cooking for her, as she still loved to do this. But he could no longer stand by correcting all the missteps; this effort was now too much for him. And so it went for a few hours, as we sifted through what would and would not work for them as a couple. We approached these concerns together and came up with a few ideas as to how the residents at Gampo Abbey might be able to help.

After our meeting, as I walked back to the monastery on the trail that Harry had forged, crossing the stream that tumbled down to the St. Lawrence Bay, I pondered what next steps I could take. After discussion with all those involved with the functioning and well-being of Gampo Abbey, we found a way to create a bit of a safety net to support Harry and Gabrielle to continue to remain in their home. Two residents from the monastery would rotate tending to Gabrielle during the day as their "work-period duties." They would alternate days so they could remain connected to the activities at Gampo Abbey. This would provide the relief Harry desperately needed. Gabrielle already knew these young people and felt at ease allowing them to help her in the kitchen and around the house. Harry and Gabrielle continued to live in their home with this arrangement for several more years. Harry became weaker over time, and he died before Gabrielle, who then moved into the home of one of her daughters, where she was cared for till her death several years later.

Their story informs how I imagine my own dance with cognitive change might play out. They showed me there can be many options to work with the adjustments that are needed. Their love and devotion to each other, and to the life they had built on the foundation of meditation and community, had given them the strength and support they needed to weather the changes in their later years. Few of us have the type of community support that Harry and Gabrielle enjoyed. But in my own search for support, I have found surprising connections within my community and circle of friends. Once someone is ready to reach out and ask for help, they are often surprised at the care and loving responses they receive.

GENEROSITY

> We don't experience the world fully unless we are willing to give everything away.
> —PEMA CHÖDRÖN, *When Things Fall Apart: Heart Advice for Difficult Times*

The most profound lesson I learned from Harry and Gabrielle was the power of generosity. Generosity is one of the six paramitas in Buddhism. The paramitas—often translated as "virtuous actions or capabilities"—are another layer of the eightfold path, as a further description of "right effort." They point to qualities that can promote a life of harmony, compassion, and openness. The six paramitas are generosity, ethical discipline, patience, heroic effort, concentration, and wisdom. The paramitas are contemplated and practiced within Buddhism in order to develop an open, warm, and compassionate heart. Just like the stages of the eightfold path, practicing any one of these paramitas strengthens all of them.

Receiving Generously

Often in Western society generosity is considered as the act of giving something away and developing nonattachment. This is an important part of working with this paramita, but there is much more to generosity than handing out money, giving gifts, and donating to a good cause. All of these are virtuous actions, but there are other aspects to generosity as well, including practicing generosity through receiving.

When I was a Buddhist nun in the late 1990s, I was only working part-time and needed additional finances in order to travel between California where my family lived and Gampo Abbey, my monastic home. Ani Pema suggested that I write a letter to sangha members asking for their support for my expenses.[4] Although it is traditional for the larger community to support monastics in this way, I hesitated. This felt like asking for a handout, which went against my upbringing that extolled a puritanical work ethic. She advised me to approach the letter writing and receiving assistance from others as a part of my practice of generosity. This turned my ideas about generosity and receiving help on its head. Asking for and accepting help became another part of realizing the interdependent nature of all relationships.

I saw this generosity of spirit in Harry and Gabrielle as they politely thanked each other as they completed each daily task, such as cooking a meal or doing the dishes. Acknowledging each act of generosity, whether you are the giver or receiver, heightens awareness of our mutuality and dependence on each other. The idea of "inter-are" shows up in so many ways in our lives. Once you begin to pay attention to these connections, you will begin to see them in so many of your daily routines and interactions. How does the smile from a grocery store cashier impact you? Do you smile back and have a lightness to your step as you leave the store? That is the reciprocal nature of a generous spirit.

Accepting Assistance

Gabrielle was generous in her acceptance of help from the young monastics as her mental capacities declined, and she opened up her home to them. Accepting this type of help can be difficult for people with cognitive issues as most of us are used to being independent in our society, and needing help can be viewed as a sign of weakness. Someone may not be aware of their growing need for aid, like David, the hospice patient I mentioned earlier. Then it is more difficult and takes some patience and sensitivity to introduce assistance when it is needed.

If one can begin to expand the concept of generosity to include receiving as well as giving, it can become a pleasure to be supported by others in the future. I have firsthand experience of this now, as I stopped driving a year ago due to issues with my vision. Driving is such an important skill in our culture, and it was a painful decision to give it up. But my friends formed a group to offer me rides using a version of the Share the Care model.

This is still a humbling situation for me, but I continue to remind myself that I am offering them an opportunity to act generously as well. These weekly rides from friends—some close and some mere acquaintances—have also offered us the time together to get to know each other better. I am sure to thank each person at the end of every ride, and they too have often thanked me for the time we have spent together. I am hoping to be able to continue this practice into the years ahead when I may not have the same level of awareness I enjoy today.

EQUAL CARING PARTNERS

The questionnaire Frank was handed for caregivers in Dr. Prichett's office suggested an unequal relationship. This may be true for us in the future, when I can no longer care for myself, but this does not match who we are at this juncture. *Care partner* is a term that better fits our relationship with each other and with this disease process. It acknowledges our equality and interdependence. We partner together in this new dance with mild cognitive impairment, just as we have partnered together to plan our garden, buy our home, and in our meditation practices. This model is what I experienced with Harry and Gabrielle, but I didn't have the words for it at that time.

Frank and I have learned some new steps together through this dance with MCI, and we will continue to shift together as more twists and turns come about over time. Remembering generosity of spirit helps guide us through whatever turbulence may come our way. My hope is that this mindset can also help others who are facing similar circumstances and changes to their abilities and independence.

If honest communication, or right speech, is the overall garden plan and self-reflection is the tool for cultivating the seeds of kindness and care, you could consider generosity as the fertilizer. By nurturing connection, openness, and warmth in communication and all our interactions with others, we can maintain a sense of equanimity, even as roles change and shift. Both the receiver and giver of care can feel respected and loved.

～

PRACTICE

Self-Reflection

Self-reflection is a skill that you can develop through formal meditation and informal practice. If you have a meditation practice, you are likely already practicing self-reflection as it tends to be a by-product of mindfulness. If you are new to self-reflection and would like to develop it outside of formal practice, or you wish to enhance your meditation through further reflection, here are a few ways that you can do this.

Journaling in the morning or evening can be one manner of reflecting on what has happened in your day, what you anticipate in the future, and your emotions and interactions with others. If this appeals to you, keeping your journal and a pen handy near your nightstand or your mug of morning coffee or tea in the morning can improve the likelihood that you will write something down. Don't worry about what you write or how you write it; this is just for you. You don't even need to use full sentences; bullet points, single words, and doodling are encouraged. I have found it helpful to review my journal notes every few months or so to track my thoughts and intentions.

Reflecting with a confidant, close friend, loved one, or therapist is another form of self-reflection. Choose someone who will not be judgmental, a person you trust that you can be totally honest with. It can help to have a regular time to check in with this person, such as once a week, so that you can both keep current with how you are doing and reflect on events as they happen. Self-reflection is a common contemplative method found in Christian and indigenous traditions.

One simple practice is to mentally review your speech and actions at the end of each day. Choose two different colored stones. For the events you considered positive, such as a kind word you shared with someone, you would choose one color of stone. For the events you considered negative, such as a fit of anger, you would choose a stone of a different color. Over time, just by doing this simple reflection each night, the positive stones will eventually outnumber the negative ones. One cautionary note about this practice: It can be heavy-handed for someone who has a propensity toward self-denigration. If you are prone to beating yourself up when your actions don't meet your expectations, stone counting may not be the best way for you to develop a positive form of self-reflection.

As you begin to pay attention to your interactions, verbal and otherwise, you may start to see some patterns and connections between what is spoken and the emotions beneath the words. Using this as a starting point, you can then expand into working intentionally with speech itself.

~

PRACTICE

Generosity

The first step in working with the paramita of generosity is through setting an aspiration. It can be a simple phrase, one that flows well for you, in your own words. Finding a phrase that you can repeat once, twice, or several times a day assists you to pay closer attention to the interactions that you engage in daily. A phrase could be something like this:

> "May my actions of giving and receiving be of benefit for myself and others."

or

> "I intend to notice when I or others are being generous today."

This first step is like hoeing the ground and planting the seeds for future actions. You will likely begin to take notice of certain acts of kindness as a result of setting this aspiration. It is a very gentle way to begin, since you are aspiring toward future change rather than judging yourself harshly for present or past deeds.

You may notice how self-reflection again is the foundation of generosity, as well as working with right speech or communication skills. Each of these tools interact together, strengthening each other. The interconnectivity of each of these practices, including the Pause Practice introduced in the first chapter, means that when you are working with any one of these concepts, you are also influencing your awareness on all these other levels at the same time. Just by choosing one of these practices to begin with will in time lead you toward the others. Allowing yourself to take these steps at your own pace is essential and one of the gifts of this eightfold path. There is no goalpost, and no particular prize for winning a race. There is a constant flow of energy within you and within all your encounters that you are learning to recognize and play with. You are literally learning to enjoy the dance.

3

Riding Emotional Waves and Finding Happiness in Everyday Life

Instead of fighting our emotions, we let them be. We simply don't act them out or repress them. We simply let them be. We simply connect with what they feel like.
—PEMA CHÖDRÖN, *How We Live Is How We Die*

A few years ago, I had the opportunity to take a road trip with my daughter, Allison, and then three-year-old granddaughter, Scarlett. As you might imagine, several days in the car with a toddler was trying at times. Our games and songs fell short of her entertainment needs, and her patience with our attempts to appease her wore thin. What amazed me most about this adventure was her ability to recognize, name, and work with her feelings. I remember a particularly loud outburst from Scarlett on the last leg of the trip as she started to wrestle with the car seat straps, tired of being bound in and at the end of her patience. My daughter was driving and I was in the back seat next to Scarlett, trying my best to calm her down.

Her cries brought up a deep anxiety in me. I tried a few distractions and wiping the tears off her face, all of which seemed to increase the intensity of her cries. My daughter said quietly to me to just let her be. Finally I resigned myself to the ear-piercing wails. But then something extraordinary happened. In between her sobs, my granddaughter gasped, "I . . . need . . . to . . . calm . . . down." My daughter replied in a soothing voice, "What do you need to calm down, Scarlett?" And to my amazement, Scarlett took a few deep breaths, then looked at me saying, "Let's look at a book now." I had just witnessed my very young granddaughter recognize and self-regulate her own emotions, something that took me more than half my adulthood to learn.

A major part of my work as a chaplain was assisting others experiencing deep and extreme emotions during a crisis. Many times I would meet a family struggling with panic, fear, and despair as their loved one was receiving emergency medical care. I needed to be an expert at regulating my own emotions during these highly charged encounters, as well as being able to support the families through their difficult emotional territory. This took years of personal emotional work and developing skills in recognizing and responding appropriately to the range of emotions people confronting uncertainty, change, and loss may experience.

It was also my job as an educator to prepare new spiritual care providers for this crucial and significant task of developing emotional intelligence, awareness, and resilience. Emotional intelligence in this context is the ability to read a room by intuiting which feelings are present and remaining openly curious and sensitive to the multiple cues, nonverbal and verbal, being communicated by patients and their families. Emotional awareness is the ability to recognize your own feelings, and resilience is the ability to work with your emotions in a way that allows you to remain grounded, present, and flexible in the middle of strong feelings and stress.

These skills—sensing others' feelings, recognizing your own feelings, and staying present to it all—are also beneficial for anyone encountering a serious life change, such as a neurodegenerative disease. How we process this new situation emotionally, and how we work with our feelings going forward, can have a direct impact on our sense of well-being and the quality of our relationships with our loved ones and care partners. I have witnessed this in a number of dementia ancestors who were able to maintain a friendly and welcoming demeanor, even when they could no longer recognize the people around them.

EMOTIONAL MEMORY AND DEMENTIA

Emotional memory and the ability to both feel and express emotions last well into the latter stages of dementia. Given this, I wondered if becoming more familiar with and knowing how to work with emotions in the early stages of cognitive change might benefit an overall sense of well-being and autonomy into the latter stages, when other forms of memory and communication might not be accessible. I have witnessed firsthand people with moderate and severe dementia continue to relate to the world through their emotions, even when they can no longer voice their thoughts, opinions, and feelings.

One dementia ancestor, Marie*, lived in a skilled nursing facility and was completely dependent on caregivers to dress and feed her. She often had a smile, although she was unable to speak. I worked as a certified nurse's aide (CNA) at the time and would rotate with others caring for Marie. She had her favorite CNAs, and when one of them would feed her lunch, she would smile, make eye contact, and willingly open her mouth, accepting the food. When one of the CNAs she disliked would try to feed her, she would close her eyes and purse her lips, refusing to take a bite, and she could not be persuaded to eat. This became so obvious that we would switch assignments at mealtimes in order to accommodate her preferences toward some CNAs over others.

Seeing this type of expression of emotional awareness by Marie and others has shown me that our emotional connections and our true nature can remain intact, and can sometimes be expressed, even when our brain no longer functions properly, communication is lost, and behaviors change drastically. By learning to ride out stormy feelings and recognize the impermanent nature of all emotion, people living with MCI and other neurodegenerative changes and their care partners may be able to improve their quality of life now and perhaps into the future.

FEELING CREATURES

When I was a teenager, my whole identity revolved around my feelings, which unconsciously influenced my thoughts and actions. If I was angry, it was someone else's fault and I would sulk for days. If I was happy, I felt invincible. My moods and decisions swung wide, riding on these emotions and the assumptions I made from them. A typical teenager, really. Like many of us, I grew into adulthood without understanding the physiology or psychology of emotions or how to work with them.

It wasn't until my late thirties that I discovered that how I feel emotionally is a powerful influence on my thoughts, actions, and physical well-being, and that my emotions are only one fleeting aspect of who I am. This was first introduced to me through my study of Buddhism, and later via psychology and neuroscience. This realization about emotions opened up a whole new way of relating to my sense of self and the world around me.

Emotional Awareness, Intelligence, and Resilience

There is much known about the positive effects of working with emotional awareness and developing emotional intelligence and resilience in the fields of psychology and neurology. Our hormones, neurons, and all our bodily functions are influenced by and interact with our emotions.

In her book *My Stroke of Insight*, Jill Bolte Taylor, a neuroanatomist, author, and public speaker, describes from a scientific and personal perspective how the brain functions on an emotional level. She recounts having a stroke, losing her ability to speak and communicate, while maintaining her awareness of what was happening. The stroke and the recovery process became a period of emotional and spiritual awakening for her. Taylor also wrote about the chemical responses of a variety of hormones to an emotional reaction that occurs automatically inside all of us.

Think of a time when you were surprised, such as when a dish slipped out of your hands, crashed to the floor, and shattered into pieces; or a time when you may have spilled a glass of orange juice on the kitchen counter. Did you feel your heart rate jump, did your face flush, or were you startled a little and your breath quickened? All of these responses are the physical reaction to hormonal shifts of adrenaline, dopamine, or serotonin, which change instantaneously when you are startled, surprised, afraid, shocked, or possibly excited. This all happens without conceptual thought; the responses are rapid and transient.

Now, the aftermath of dropping the dish on the floor can bring up a multitude of thoughts and feelings, including anger, regret, shame, or even humor. However, the hormonal surge through our entire body only lasts ninety seconds, according to Taylor. The emotion and our physiological response to it will end after a minute and a half unless we feed it through thoughts and preoccupation. This is when we often perpetuate storylines and ongoing feelings that extend the emotional and physical response for longer than the initial ninety seconds.

This insight revolutionized how I relate to my feelings, loosening the all-too-familiar sense of being carried away by my own emotional reactions to life's challenges. Realizing the basic physiology of how hormones and emotions are connected and interact has been freeing. I began to wonder, "What happens when I allow myself to feel the physical response running its course without adding any additional thoughts to the event?"

This is where choice comes in and we can decide consciously how we wish to respond, beyond our initial automatic reaction. About a year ago, when I was beginning to have vision issues and a small tremor, I accidentally knocked my glass teapot onto the floor. It shattered into tiny fragments of tea-soaked glass. I stood in the middle of the kitchen, stunned and upset. I wanted to place blame somewhere, and I began to chastise myself for being so clumsy while I started to mop up the mess. Through a few tears, while I dumped the dustpan full of broken glass in the trash, I caught myself getting hooked by the insults I was throwing at myself. Then I took a few deep breaths, re-membering that this new clumsiness is a part of my changing abilities, not an intentional act. I still felt sad about losing my favorite teapot, but the overlay of self-hate dissolved.

WEATHERING EMOTIONS

The scientific understanding of emotions is also reflected in Buddhist teachings that have been practiced for thousands of years. The Bud-dha's enlightenment story mirrors this attitude toward emotions, as he faced a night filled with temptations and terror. Being able to stay present, grounded, and unphased during this deluge of distractions and strong emotions was the final step toward his full awakening. In Tibetan Buddhism, the emotions are described through the basic elements of earth, air, fire, water, and space. Our everyday language reveals this connection between the natural elements and emotions when we use phrases like "a flare-up of anger" or "a wave of sadness." These common expressions also illustrate the variety of emotions and the different intensities of those emotions we can experience, from the warmth of a stove to the rage of a blazing wildfire.

One of my first introductions to Buddhism was in 1993 through Pema Chödrön's book *The Wisdom of No Escape*. Chödrön devotes a chapter—"Weather and the Four Noble Truths"—to the topic of working with our emotions by using the Buddhist path. Her analogy of emotions as weather deeply resonated, as I often experienced my feelings sweeping through me like a windstorm. Consider emotions as an expression of our aliveness, the life force that animates all liv-ing creatures. This energy is what makes us a "creature of feeling that thinks," as Taylor suggests. We can learn to recognize and tolerate the intense heat of anger over time rather than feeding this emotion with our stories, which can potentially harm ourselves and others.

If this is so, I wondered, "Why do we resist feeling those feelings when they come up?" I have at times felt overwhelmed by my own emotions. A tidal wave of fear, sadness, or depression can feel unrelenting and all consuming. What I have learned is that the more I resist these emotions—the good and the bad—the more intense they become, the more solid they seem to be, and the less I can stay present.

In the moments when I can rest in the middle of an emotional earthquake, such as a sudden and fatal diagnosis of a loved one, I can ride out the ground shaking beneath my feet. When I can breathe slowly and allow the emotions of anger, sadness, or resentment to just be, their hold on me loosens. As the fabric of the feeling loosens, there are tiny gaps between its threads. These gaps allow some ventilation where other textures of feeling may appear or a change in perspective might arise. This is when we may become aware that the energy of these emotions shift, just as the energy of being alive is ever changing.

Emotions are fluid, not solid and fixed. These are moments when there is the potential to connect with our true nature, which includes the full kaleidoscope of emotions. Through allowing the feeling to soften, there is the opportunity to recognize that each one of us has the ability to connect with this energy directly. Love, joy, compassion, and equanimity, which are called the qualities of an open heart, are the underlying container for this emotional weather system also comprising grief, excitement, anger, and frustration.

Clinical depression is a mood disorder that can make it very difficult to work with emotions in the manner that I am describing.

Chemical changes within the brain of someone who has clinical depression could make this type of emotional work nearly impossible. Depression can often accompany neurocognitive decline, leading to a constant feeling of sadness or a lack of ambition. Medical and psychological support can assist a person with serious depression, in which case, emotional awareness might become more accessible over time.

Learning how to allow the fluidity of feelings to move through us and dissipate builds emotional resilience and strengthens our ability to weather any emotional storm with a little more ease. The Pause Practice, introduced in the first chapter, is one way to work with strong emotions, allowing a bit of space and time to become familiar with what we are experiencing in the moment, whether that is the openness and relaxation of feeling happy, like a warm summer breeze, or the cold, blustering winds of confusion and worry.

Suggestions from a scientific perspective and the Buddhist view are essentially identical. When a strong feeling arises, especially one that seems to occur often for you, first acknowledge it as a guest at your door and let it be. In other words, allow yourself to experience the feeling without adding any story to it or pushing it away. Where do you feel it in your body? Is it solid or fluid? Can you stay with the raw energy of that emotion?

Next, do something different.

We all have habitual emotional patterns—certain ways we react to our feelings. When the dish hits the floor, do you immediately feel anger or shame? It's human to initially react to the shock of the moment in that first gasp of breath, perhaps even with a word you wish you wouldn't use. But can you then pause, after the sudden shock, and choose in the next moment to respond in a new way?

Recently I had a situation like this. I have become quite clumsy lately, often dropping or knocking things over. The last time I spilled a drink all over the counter, I started berating myself as I reached for the towel. This is one of my typical reactions. But by the time I was mopping up my mess, I had taken a few deep breaths and found myself marveling at the pattern of the juice as it curled around the spice rack, instead of continuing to belittle myself. The spill became an ordinary occurrence as I let go of the internal dialogue, remembering to rest in the uniqueness of this particular moment without the storyline. I can't always do this, but when I can, there is a sense of freshness and freedom. In this way, any event can become an opportunity to strengthen internal flexibility and resilience rather than becoming another time of perpetuating self-reproach or anger.

Allowing an emotion to flow through you is different from repressing or pushing away a feeling. Here you relax into the feel of it completely and yet do not hold on to it or extend it. This is similar to the old adage to count to ten when you are angry. If you grit your teeth and ruminate the whole time you are counting, it will likely increase your rage. But if you can relax, breathe, and feel the anger, it will begin to ease and shift. Some emotions can be very strong and you may feel them rolling through you, wave after wave, but you can still experience a gap between each wave.

Working with Emotions

Using the Pause Practice and then choosing to do something different is one strategy for working with your emotions, becoming more familiar with your own responses and strengthening a sense of agency. However, I don't want to be misleading. This is not an easy practice. It is a practice of missing the mark over and over. When we begin to pay attention to our emotions, we first catch the afterglow, perhaps through reflecting on the day or through feedback from others. Over time, we can begin to catch the feelings as they arise.

It is important to remember the foundational practices of loving-kindness and patience with yourself when working with emotions. This is a lifetime endeavor of becoming more intimate with and accepting of our own emotional patterns through applying attention and intention over and over again. It can be useful to have someone you trust that you can talk to about what you are discovering as you explore your emotional world. A spouse, friend, spiritual leader, chaplain, spiritual director, or therapist are some options you may wish to consider for support if you choose to undertake this internal journey.

This discussion about working with emotions barely scratches the surface of the information and techniques that can be used to develop emotional intelligence, awareness, and resiliency. If you are curious and interested in learning more, please see the resources at the back of the book.

Quality of Life

It seems to me that the early stage of MCI is not only an opportunity to develop emotional intelligence, awareness, and resilience but also a time to increase the daily activities that bring a sense of calm, peace, and happiness. Developing habits and hobbies that someone enjoys now can support the person living with the disease and those who are caring for them now and potentially into the future.

Dr. Linda Lam, MBChB, MD, professor from Chinese University of Hong Kong, gave a plenary talk during the 2022 Alzheimer's Association International Conference. The focus of her research and talk was not on a cure or prevention of neurodegenerative disease but rather the quality of life for the individual living with the disease and their care partners throughout the journey into dementia.

Her research followed people with MCI and early dementia over decades as their disease progressed into severe dementia. What she found was those who had developed positive habits and things that they enjoyed earlier in their life or even during the early stages in their disease process appeared to have a greater quality of life later on than those who did not. Quality of life includes enjoyment of activities and an overall sense of contentment and well-being.

Dr. Lam gave an example of a woman she met who was in the early stages of Alzheimer's disease. This woman loved completing five-hundred-piece jigsaw puzzles. This was something that she did every day for hours. Over the years she was no longer able to put the pieces in the correct place, but she still enjoyed working with the puzzle a few hours each day. It was the act of working with the pieces that mattered. Her son, who cared for her, also found it rewarding to see her happily occupied each day.

Dr. Lam has collaborated with researchers throughout Asia who are conducting studies of people with MCI engaging in calligraphy, dance, meditation, and music. All these activities seem to have a similar effect of extending the person's enjoyment and improving their quality of life throughout the stages of cognitive change. Researchers are evaluating whether these activities actually slow cognitive decline, but their findings are not yet conclusive at the time of this writing.

There are several lifestyle changes that are medically recommended for slowing down the progression of neurodegenerative disease, such as exercise, diet, good sleep habits, socialization, and cognitive stimulation. But none of these practices focus specifically on quality of life. Dr. Lam suggests that if a person does not enjoy the suggested lifestyle changes, they will have difficulty maintaining these changes for the months, years, and decades necessary to continue to slow the disease process. If a person can combine pleasure with the positive lifestyle recommendations, they are more likely to continue these habits for years to come, both enhancing cognition and an overall sense of contentment. Dr. Lam gave the example of dance, an activity many people enjoy. It is often aerobic while exercising cognitive function in order to coordinate movement with the music, and it is a social activity.

How to pair pleasure with the suggested lifestyle changes to slow cognitive decline is a very personal question worth asking. Perhaps taking a dance lesson if you enjoy dancing, listening to a podcast on a topic of interest, hiking a trail, or trying a new recipe that supports a healthy diet suits you better. Whatever it is that excites you and supports the health of your brain is a win-win.

Behavioral and physical issues separate from memory—such as a shift in a person's personality, social withdrawal, or speech and balance issues not typical for the person prior to the disease—can be a part of neurological changes. Dr. Lam suggests the positive habits that one enjoys may have a buffering effect on these behavioral issues, though they may not be mitigated completely. Currently, new treatment plans are being developed based on understanding some of the behavior changes common for people living with dementia to assist with issues such as nonverbal expressions of fear or pain. This will be explored further in chapter 7, "Living with Grace amid Paradox and Unpredictability."

TOM

Tom*, another dementia ancestor, was just beginning to have some aggressive behavior issues when I first met him. He still lived at home with his wife, Beth*. Beth had been his sole caregiver for many years, but she was becoming isolated as his aggressive behavior intensified. Tom was nonverbal at this time and did not like to be left alone in a room. He often didn't understand what was going on around him, such as cooking, and would become impatient. Sometimes he seemed angry and would push past Beth or me while we were trying to assist him with dressing or personal care.

Initially Beth asked me to stay with Tom a few hours several times a week so that she could take time to play cards with her friends. Often when Beth left, Tom would appear confused, pacing back and forth from the front door to the living room, looking for her. He did not respond well if I tried to intervene to help him calm down. He would push past me and seem even more upset. I learned to quietly turn on the television to one of his favorite shows and sit down in the living room during these episodes. After a few minutes, Andy Griffith or Barney Fife would catch his attention. Before long, he would settle down into his recliner to watch TV with me, now in a calmer state of mind. This is an example of how an activity Tom enjoyed aided him in coping with the stress of his wife's absence, even though he was nonverbal and could sometimes be aggressive.

Apathy, depression, and extreme anxiety are more difficult symptoms of neurodegenerative disease that may hinder a person's ability to enjoy activities that they once favored. If this is the case for you or your loved one, it may be helpful to consult with a health-care provider in order to address these symptoms from multiple angles.

Improving one's quality of life may not change the course of the illness, but it may ease the journey, increasing your enjoyment of the present moment and creating more times of happiness, love, and fulfillment. As Dr. Prichett so wisely reminded me when I was first diagnosed, essentially this present moment is all we can count on, so why not live it to the fullest extent that we can.

MOTIVATION TO CHANGE

Change is not easy. It takes motivation to create positive and long-lasting changes in one's life at any stage, but it can be even more challenging when dealing with the effects of mild cognitive impairment. Becoming clear about what is motivating you to make the changes you decide to focus on can help. If you begin to lose your excitement to continue a new activity, a strong motivation can act as a reminder as to why you felt it was important in the first place. From a Buddhist perspective, there are three different levels of motivation. Each is a good motivator alone, and the three often overlap, enhancing one another. Working with these categories might assist you in identifying your motivations. The stronger the motivation, the more likely you are to pursue your desired changes for the long term.

The first level of motivation is to help yourself. Given the impact of MCI on one's life, understanding the personal benefits of a particular activity is a very important aspect of motivation. Perhaps you wish to commit to a regular exercise routine. Knowing that aerobic exercise is stimulating for the brain and can potentially slow cognitive decline as well as improve your physical well-being and stamina can be a strong motivating factor.

The second level of motivation, the wish to help others, can be a motivating factor for working with your emotions. Helping others can assist you in understanding yourself at a deeper level and also improve communication with others, leading to more openness and responsiveness in your relationships with your friends and loved ones.

The third level of motivation is based on an unselfish concern for others. The desire to act compassionately to help those beyond our circle of loved ones is a form of altruism. We all possess an innate capacity to feel compassion toward others. Our motivation to be of benefit for all beings can be a natural expression of our interconnectedness with those who may be suffering. A person's faith may inform and encourage this altruistic attitude, though no faith is necessary to want to reach out and help someone. This level of motivation may lead one to volunteer to raise money for a cause, educate the public about an issue, or join a clinical study, knowing that you may not benefit from these actions yourself but that others in the future will. Altruistic activities connect us with the larger world and allow us to have a sense of purpose and belonging, even when our abilities are declining. We can still make a difference and bring meaning into our lives.

You can see how these three levels of motivation can go hand in hand. Like intertwined concentric circles, each level of motivation can strengthen the others. Improving sleep habits is one of the lifestyle changes physicians recommend. This is an area where I struggle, as my sleeping patterns are sporadic, with many sleepless hours in the middle of the night. As a part of addressing this personal issue, I find it helpful to remember an altruistic approach. When lying in bed trying to fall asleep, I repeat to myself, "May tonight's sleep and dreams be of benefit for myself and all others." This combined motivation is very nurturing and cultivates feelings of appreciation, love, and joy for me, as it is a call to care for myself, my loved ones, and all beings, all at once.

WHERE'S THE JOY?

When I first began reading articles and books about mild cognitive impairment and the road toward dementia, I was surprised at the tone of much of the writing. It seemed to lack any references to happiness. Finding joy in small moments of beauty and grace in my day-to-day life is what helps sustain me and is the foundation for maintaining my sense of compassion, openness, and connection with others. Enjoying the seemingly mundane moments by paying attention to details, such as the smell of freshly brewed coffee or the mottled sunlight sifting through tree branches, means happiness is at my fingertips anytime I look up and out at the world around me. I wondered if there was room to experience this type of joy in life even while losing cognitive abilities. The advice from my teachers and the lessons I've learned from my dementia ancestors guide my exploration of the open question: Where's the joy?

> Be happy with no particular reason
> —DZIGAR KONGTRUL RINPOCHE

The Tibetan Buddhist teacher and author Dzigar Kongtrul Rinpoche invites us to look at happiness and joy in a new light. To think about just being happy, without a direct cause, is a revolutionary idea. When I remember this message, I can enjoy the sheer beauty of being alive and become more aware of the world through all of my senses. It is a reminder to take a moment to feel gratitude and happiness for the small moments when I can relax and discover a little bit of joy for no particular reason.

Mary*, one of my dementia ancestors, modeled this love of life and was able to maintain it through her decline into the end stages of dementia. When I first met Mary, she was still living at home but struggled to cook and take her medications, and she would sometimes wander and get lost. I helped care for Mary in her home until she needed to move into a facility. She was a strong woman who had raised a large family and farmed the land for most of her life. Although she was very independent, she accepted my assistance with warmth and kindness. We had many times of laughter together, even as her dementia was advancing and she was quickly becoming more dependent and reliant on others.

I remember one day when she sent me out to the garden to harvest an armful of rhubarb stalks. I had never cooked rhubarb before and was unsure what to do with it. Mary was delighted to talk me through the process of making rhubarb syrup. She had a mischievous glint in her eye as she poured the sugar until it overflowed onto the tablecloth. We mixed the chopped stalks, water, and sugar together and turned up the country music from her favorite radio station. As the rhubarb and sugar concoction simmered, we danced around the kitchen together, smiling and laughing, as the sweet smell of the syrup filled the room. I don't think anyone could have ever been happier than she was that afternoon. We danced until we were out of breath, and she sat down hard on the kitchen chair. She wore a big grin and was chuckling, ready for some warm rhubarb syrup over vanilla ice cream. It was the most delicious dessert I have ever eaten.

Mary had this quality about her throughout the time I knew her, including in her final years when she lived in a skilled nursing facility. Whenever I would visit, she had that broad smile and the glint of mischief in her eye. She no longer knew who I was, and she wasn't able to say very much, but she did not lose her sense of humor and kind nature.

Pema provided invaluable spiritual guidance for me after my diagnosis of MCI. Part of this advice included offering up every experience—good, bad, and neutral—for the universal well-being of all beings. One day last fall, soon after I received Pema's advice, Frank and I went for a hike. It was a glorious day. The sun was warm, the sky was a deep blue, and the leaves were just beginning to show their colors of orange and red. As we walked up to a ridge overlooking the Mississippi River, I silently offered the beauty of the environment and the contentment I felt to all beings. I created a personal silent ritual by pausing, taking a deep breath as I took in the beauty around me and thought of all those who might benefit from a moment of peace. I offered all this up using a single, silent word: "Enjoy." This simple ritual gave me a deep feeling of connection and happiness.

Focusing on joy and offering it out to others may sound a bit eccentric, but the act of being joyful and benevolent has a positive effect biologically, psychologically, and spiritually. When we are happy, certain hormones are released in our brain and pulse through our body.

These hormones, known as endorphins and dopamine, calm anxiety, decrease painful sensations, and help us sleep better. When we are happy or joyful, our heart and mind are more open and receptive to others. This can be both a psychological and spiritual experience, as it can ease anxiety and worry as well as connect us with a greater understanding of our meaning and purpose.

Joy is closely akin to gratitude. Gratitude can be a wonderful antidote for self-pity and worry. Expressing gratitude on a daily basis can create a sense of connection with others and a feeling of contentment within yourself. The simplicity of saying thank you for the preparation of a meal, at the end of a friend's visit, or any occasion when someone has assisted you can bolster you and the receiver. Cultivating gratitude and joy may not change a situation, but it can shift how we perceive and respond to our circumstances.

I feel happy when I offer moments of contentment to others, and it reminds me how we are all connected. My happiness can be shared with you. You can share your happiness with others too. This is a universal expression of openness and kindness that goes beyond religious boundaries. Anyone can try this to experiment and see for yourself, How do you feel when you offer the moments in your life that you value most to others?

FLEXIBILITY AND ADJUSTMENT

When I was young, I studied several types of dance. I spent hours stretching and repeating dance steps over and over. It was an activity that I loved, and I slowly developed some dancing skills and physical flexibility. What I didn't realize at the time, I was also growing new neurons and taking advantage of what is called neuroplasticity while preparing for my next dance performance.

Neuroplasticity is a fancy way of saying that the brain can create new neural pathways as we repeat an activity, such as when we are learning something new. I think of this as being similar to how a hiking path develops near the river. At first it is difficult to see, and there can be a lot of overgrowth making it hard to follow. Gradually, the more it is used, the easier that path becomes to follow. The same is true in our brain.

Say you decide to learn a new language. At first the words are foreign and you may stumble trying to get through the lesson. With time and practice, the basic words become easier to remember. Your brain has created a new path that allows this kind of learning. It turns out you can teach an old dog new tricks! Cognitive decline can make it more difficult to learn something new, but it is not impossible, especially in the early stages, before dementia begins.

Neuroplasticity means that our neurons are more flexible than neuroscience used to think. This flexibility may help buffer some of the impact of neurodegenerative disease early on, making it easier to adjust as cognition changes, although it does not alter the overall trajectory. A simple example is starting to use sticky notes to keep track of appointments and tasks. This tactic is often helpful for people with MCI and is likely a new habit formed out of necessity.

Tom and Mary both adjusted in different ways to their changing needs and abilities. Mary accepted my help in making the rhubarb syrup when she could no longer cook it herself. Tom learned that he could relax and watch *The Andy Griffith Show* with me while his wife was gone.

Today, instead of dance classes I take yoga, as I hung up my tap shoes years ago. I particularly enjoy the twisting poses. In these positions, legs are wrapped around the body in unlikely shapes and you are twisting the torso so that you're nearly looking behind yourself. My teacher likes to point out how this gives us a new perspective on life as well as develops flexibility in our spine. Can we adjust and find a new outlook or create new neural pathways now, so that we continue to show up in our lives the best we can in each moment?

One hospice patient comes to mind, whom I visited regularly in a residential care facility in California. She had advanced dementia and was nonverbal when I met her. As she became bedbound and approaching the end of her life, her family shared with me that she was an avid Bible reader and devoted Christian. At my last visit, I read Psalm 23 to her as a form of prayer. Although she was not able to move at all at this point, her eyes were open and fixed on me as I read. Then one tear rolled down her cheek. As a chaplain, I try not to put my own interpretation on someone else's experience. I really don't know what she was thinking or feeling at that moment, but there seemed to be some thread of recognition from hearing the psalm to her many years of faith, which I hope was meaningful for her and provided some comfort.

My tap shoes no longer fit me, but I still enjoy dancing in the kitchen to my favorite tunes while cleaning the counters, and I hope to keep tapping my toes to the music of the 1960s and 1970s for decades to come.

However, none of this is to be misunderstood as a self-improvement project. The main difference between the mindset of self-improvement and applying the practices suggested in this chapter and throughout the book is that this is a path of waking up to the intrinsic nature of self-love, compassion, and joy, which is the essence of who you already are. There is no need to add anything. Rather, tune in to your internal wisdom, happiness, and passion for life. Let that be your guide.

You may decide to become more familiar with your emotions, increasing emotional intelligence and resiliency. You may choose to create a personal ritual focusing on daily moments of joy. However you decide to engage your mind and body, you have the chance to care for more than the health of your brain. As you extend this to include others in your thoughts, prayers, and heart, you are creating compassion and openness, which can nurture you spiritually and support a sense of meaning and purpose in your life and the lives of those around you.

My hope is that you feel fully immersed in life and keep tapping your toes to your favorite tunes as you go forward into the unknown future with gentleness, patience, and determination.

PRACTICE

Compassionate Abiding

Compassionate abiding is another form of on-the-spot meditation Pema teaches as a way to work with uncomfortable emotions.

When you find you are suffering—which means you are experiencing any sort of discomfort, such as feeling tight, angry, or anxious—breathe this feeling into your heart center. Acknowledge and accept it, surrendering to and embracing the feeling as best you can.

As you breathe in, feel your heart center expand to accommodate the emotion. When you breathe out, allow there to be a sense of spaciousness and openness.

Repeat this process three to six times in the moment.

Eventually, you may wish to extend the practice to connecting with all beings that are suffering from the same feelings. This practice helps you to accept yourself and the situation just as it is.

4

Untangling Bias and Stigma with Clarity and Loving-Kindness

BIAS: noun 1. prejudice in favor of or against one thing, person, or group compared with another, usually in a way considered to be unfair.

verb 1. cause to feel or show inclination or prejudice for or against someone or something.

STIGMA: noun 1. a mark of disgrace associated with a particular circumstance, quality, or person.

—*OXFORD DICTIONARY*

Bias and stigma go hand in hand and have an impact consciously and unconsciously in many levels of our social and personal lives. Bias against those with cognitive issues is common in our society and often results in the person with cognition issues feeling shame and additional fear and anxiety through being stigmatized. Plenty of anxiety and fear come naturally with a serious diagnosis such as mild cognitive impairment, but biases add an additional social and personal burden for the person with the disease and their loved ones.

At the end of my first clinical study two years ago, Frank and I waited in a tiny, sterile exam room for the doctor to come and talk to us about the results. We waited an hour for a ten-minute conversation. The doctor and his assistant entered and stood near the door. Frank sat on a wheeled stool, wedged between the examining table and the wall, and I sat in a recliner designed for intravenous infusions, with such a deep seat my feet didn't reach the floor. The doctor spoke directly to Frank, asking him if I was still functioning independently. Gratefully, Frank didn't answer but looked to me, and I responded emphatically, "Yes." The doctor then told us, still focusing on Frank, that the neurological testing and the PET scan, which was positive for an elevated amyloid level, pointed toward mild cognitive impairment, due to Alzheimer's disease. I felt ignored and frustrated by the physician's behavior; he continued to look past me as if I had no understanding of what was being said in this brief and disrespectful interaction. That was my first but not my last experience of feeling the stigma of the MCI diagnosis.

BUDDHA NATURE

Most religions and indigenous wisdom traditions include a philosophy that each of us have an innate capacity for love and compassion within our hearts. In Buddhism, the idea that each individual possesses these qualities and has the potential to discover and cultivate them is called buddha nature. An innate capacity for love and compassion is also a key concept within Christian teachings. In the Bible Jesus said, "Behold, the kingdom of God is within you."[5] Dzigar Kongtrul Rinpoche defines buddha nature as "the innate qualities of warmth, intelligence, and openness which resides in all beings."[6]

The view that all sentient beings hold a core of basic goodness, like a seed that just needs some nurturing in order to grow to its full potential, is a guiding light for how I relate to the world. I try to remember this during uncomfortable circumstances, such as that meeting with the doctor. Although I was pained by the physician's actions and the long wait we endured for such a brief meeting, I wondered what background training he had in compassionate communication and what his day had been like before he came in to meet with us. None of this excuses his lack of skill in that moment but rather considers that there was more going on for him in that moment than I could be aware of.

Working with the notion that we are all blessed with the innate traits of kindness, love, and compassion and that we all wish to be happy and free from suffering, softens my perception of others. This helps me to remain a little more open and accepting of others in the moment. It loosened my sense of resentment toward the doctor, although this took some time to settle into. Tapping into this source of compassion, love, and joy can help transform challenging situations into opportunities to experience connection within ourselves and with others.

For most of us, this seed of basic goodness has been covered over by our habitual tendencies that appear to protect us but actually disconnect us from others and our own open tenderheartedness. These habitual tendencies are a natural part of being human, but if we don't examine them and determine for ourselves what is helpful and what is harmful, we can go through our lives without realizing our own capacity for loving-kindness. This is a radical form of self-acceptance and openness to the beauty within all of us, even when that beauty might be shadowed by anger, jealousy, greed, or ignorance.

Imagine thinking about your loved ones, your friends, and the strangers you meet as each one holding the gems of love and compassion in their heart. You can even take this to the next level and consider politicians, global leaders, those suffering through catastrophes and violence around the world, or your grumpy neighbor next door all having this same basic goodness within their hearts. Sometimes it is easier to see this in animals than we can in our fellow humans. If you have an animal companion such as a cat or dog, I imagine you are well aware of their ability to show you love and affection.

This basic goodness within yourself and others is important to remember as we examine the biases and stigma that can be so hurtful personally and socially. Understanding that these negative perspectives are covering over a heart of kindness we all share can assist in looking at the issues of bias and stigma with eyes wide open and allow for true change to occur on intrapersonal and interpersonal levels. This understanding helps me recognize when biased thoughts come up in my own mind and encourages me to look at them with care for myself and for the person I am feeling biased toward.

HISTORICAL ROOTS

Most biases have historical roots that carry weight into current thoughts and beliefs. Many social movements today are working toward exposing these roots and changing systems of oppression and misinformation. We also need to expose the roots of stigmatization of individuals with cognitive changes and/or mental illness. Cognitive changes and mental illness are two separate categories, though they can be related and were often considered one and the same historically.

Neurocognitive issues relate specifically to structural issues of the brain itself, such as the buildup of the proteins amyloid and tau, and the death of neurons. These changes can be seen on PET scans and MRIs. Mental health conditions are changes in mood, thinking, and behavior, which are brought about by chemical imbalances within the brain and environmental pressures such as trauma, abuse, chronic stress, and systemic marginalization. Some mental health conditions are also a part of neurodegenerative disease through the physical changes within the brain, like depression, anxiety, and apathy. Mood changes can also be a part of a psychological response to a terminal disease that is feared and shunned by most of our society.

I found myself wondering, "Why is there such a negative bias toward Alzheimer's disease and other forms of dementia?" This curiosity led me to research the origins of this culturally pervasive stigma and fear in order to better understand the current attitudes toward neurodegenerative disease.[7]

Dementia has been described throughout human history with evidence recorded back to the Egyptians around 2000 B.C.E. At that time it was expected that if a person lived into their later years, age seventy or more at that time, they would have declining mental capacity and eventually would fall into a state similar to a "suckling infant."[8] During the Roman Empire, it was recognized that not everyone who lived into old age developed dementia. At this time, mental decline was considered a result of an individual's weak will. The Middle Ages brought condemnation of those with dementia. It was thought to be a punishment from God or a sign of witchcraft. Many people with dementia were burned at the stake as witches. Cognitive impairment became a condition of shame to hide away, since acknowledging this disease could lead to a death sentence.

Dementia was accepted as a medical diagnosis in 1797, but Alzheimer's disease was not recognized as a distinct illness until 1910. Even with this advancement, dementia was considered a form of insanity well into the 1950s. Many elders were committed to state mental institutions. Around this time, there was also a shift within the study of psychiatry toward framing dementia as a psychosocial problem, challenging the notion of institutionalization. This led to a call for social programs to provide care and support outside of mental hospitals. In 1953, Jerome Kaplan, an advocate for social programs, argued,

> With the number of people who are over 65 increasing significantly each year, our society is today finding itself faced with the problem of keeping a large share of its population from joining the living dead—those whose minds are allowed to die before their bodies do.[9]

This new view of aging and dementia as a social issue led to policy changes, such as the creation of the Medicare program. As recent as 1970, dementia was declared a major public health issue, and a coalition of caregivers and family members pushed for the recognition that these cognitive changes originate from a disease process rather than a part of normal aging. This raised a call for more research funding.

Unfortunately there was an unexpected backlash in the 1970s from lobbying for more research focused on finding a cure; offering education, support, and care for those afflicted with neurodegenerative disease, their families, and caregivers was neglected.

In order to make the case that Alzheimer's causes great suffering, advocates represented the losses associated with dementia as so total and irrevocable as to call into question whether
people suffering from it could still properly be regarded as
people at all, thus greatly deepening the stigmatization of
those diagnosed with it and intensifying the anxiety people
felt about aging itself.[10]

This backlash prompted the development of organizations, such as
the Alzheimer's Association, to provide the information and support
required for families to care for their loved ones with the disease. The
Alzheimer's Association was founded in 1980 and has grown into an
international organization focused on support and research providing
education for those facing dementia, their loved ones, and caregivers.
The association is also a strong advocate for addressing the need for
public education and understanding.[11]

Within the last few decades, researchers have made great strides,
including a greater understanding of the physiological changes leading to neurodegenerative disease. This has led to suggested preventative lifestyle changes to slow the progression and the potential of
some promising early diagnosis and treatments. New medications to
slow the decline of MCI and early Alzheimer's are just now coming
onto the market. Beyond the field of pharmaceuticals, research-based
programs offer improved compassionate care through a better understanding of the behavioral issues often present with moderate and severe dementia.

However, with all the medical research and increased understanding about neurodegenerative diseases, some people still relate

dementia with a lack of willpower, a spiritual punishment, or a mental illness. Strong carryovers from generations of misinformation, myths, and biases have endured for centuries.

It should be noted that several indigenous cultures do not regard cognitive changes in the same way that Western culture does. Some of these cultures tend to be geared toward multigenerational living, consider cognitive issues as a natural fact of life, and treat people with dementia with compassionate care within the home.

UNCONSCIOUS BIAS

We all have biases—more simply put, likes and dislikes. Generally when using the term *bias*, we think of a negative connotation toward a group of people or an individual. Often these are attitudes we learned early that have historical roots we have little awareness of, unless we begin to challenge some of our underlying assumptions about ourselves and others. Self-deprecation is rampant in the internal dialogues of many people in Western culture, as are negative opinions and skepticism toward those who are different from us. These tendencies undermine the warmth and goodness of humanity we all share. These unconscious inclinations cause a great deal of pain for ourselves and others, individually and at every level of society.

It takes a strong resolve, gentleness, and courage to begin to dismantle the undercurrent of unconscious thoughts. In order to begin to shift one's mindset, opening the door for growth and acceptance, one must first bring awareness to what that mindset is.

Entering into Clinical Pastoral Education (CPE) in the year 2000 began my personal introspection about unknown biases I held and how they impacted my ministry with patients. CPE programs are designed to facilitate this type of self-reflection, which became a powerful tool for my personal development as a professional chaplain. I had just given back my monastic vows, but I still shaved my head and preferred to wear maroon, habits from life at the monastery I wasn't quite ready to give up. It had been years since I worked in a hospital as a nurse, and entering as a chaplain resident was an entirely new and unexplored avenue for me.

In this new environment, using an experiential learning process known as an action/reflection model, I quickly became aware that I was undermining some of my patient visits before even getting in the door. During one of my presentations to my peer group and educator about my patient visits, I realized that I tended to ignore or cut short visits with male patients but not with female patients. Through the group discussion it became obvious I held an unconscious bias against visiting men.

I was surprised to realize this, but I could quickly see how this affected my ministry. There were deeper issues of past trauma, male authority, shyness, and insecurity tied up in this internal bias that needed to be addressed. Once this inclination was revealed, I could do something about it. This was one of my first personal experiences of recognizing the power of unconscious bias. Then it was up to me to decide what and how to change my behavior. Recognition of a personal bias is the most important step in dismantling it. I grew to recognize when my bias with men would come up during my work and I could then consciously take steps to soothe my uneasiness. By taking a slow, deep breath before entering the room and maintaining an open, positive attitude when meeting any new patient, this tendency to avoid male patients quickly dissipated.

Since my diagnosis of mild cognitive impairment, I have looked back at my earlier attitude when I was a caregiver for my dear dementia ancestors. I realize now that I had internalized the predominant social stigma and held my own biases about the capabilities of my dementia ancestors. I had no idea what my patients were experiencing, though I hope they still felt cared for. Social issues contributed to my ignorance in this regard, as well as a lack of medical knowledge at the time. From where I stand now, I have a new level of compassion and empathy for those who are so misunderstood. And here I am, now confronting this same disease process.

This form of reminiscence is a part of the process of untangling bias and stigma within ourselves. By doing this internal work, we can then be prepared to confront and facilitate social change, beginning with the circle of our family and friends. Just like working with emotions, working with unconscious attitudes takes time and gentleness. First, one needs to be open and willing to look at those unexamined thoughts as they arise. Then it takes a bit of curiosity and loving-kindness to question where that thought comes from and if it's true. This reminds me of a popular bumper sticker, "Don't believe everything you think!"

STIGMA

Mild cognitive impairment is often an invisible disease. I have received comments from friends that are well meaning but insensitive, such as "But you look fine," "I forget things sometimes too," and "You seem okay to me." I don't believe that these statements are meant to be derogatory; they are intended to empathize and normalize my experience. When this happens, I can feel misunderstood, frustrated, and unheard. It puts me in the position of having to defend my diagnosis and educate those around me about the impact of MCI and the difference between normal aging and more-than-normal cognitive decline. This is a very personal effect of the long-standing social biases and lack of public understanding. It seems that as a person with this diagnosis, I have two choices: I can hide away and keep these changes to myself, or I can be vocal about my own experience and advocate for more awareness and understanding of this disease, one conversation at a time. This contributed to my inspiration to write this book.

Feeling dismissed is not unique to me. Many people with MCI or other cognitive issues face similar situations when they feel misunderstood. I have learned to think carefully about how and when to tell someone about these new health issues. Over time and through many conversations I have come to expect certain initial reactions from my friends and acquaintances. First there is dismay and disbelief. "Not you!" exclaimed one dear friend. I silently wondered, "Why not me?" For my friend, knowing that I was diagnosed with a neurodegenerative disease meant that this could happen to her too. This was too close to home for her comfort, and she felt threatened by my diagnosis and saddened about the implied changes to our future relationship.

I hear this fear and worry echoed in other comments when I describe some of my symptoms. Often this is met with, "Oh, I do that too." Although this seemed dismissive to me at first, now when I hear similar statements, I ask the person more about what they mean and

what they are experiencing. Sometimes it turns out that they have serious concerns about their own memory but have been afraid to talk
about it. Then the door opens up for us to have an honest conversation about their concerns and steps they can take to address them.

About a year ago, I was just beginning to share my diagnosis with
others. I had the opportunity to speak privately with a friend who has a
background as a psychotherapist. As I described my diagnosis and the
long-term implications, he began to argue with me about the diagnosis
itself. He was suggesting that MCI was just a "label" put on a psychological issue that I could likely address through more meditation and talk
therapy. I was surprised at this response and again felt the frustration
and stigma of being misunderstood, but I was open to continuing the
debate because I cherish his friendship. Then I asked him if he would
try to talk a cancer patient out of their diagnosis. He responded quickly,
"Of course not." I took a deep breath and continued, "So, why are you
trying to talk me out of a diagnosis that is based on physical changes
in the brain?" This was an aha moment for him and a shift in his tone.
Now he was able to listen to what I was trying to explain to him without
the bias that this was all in my head. Pun intended! Humor is a great
antidote when having these kinds of discussions about MCI. If I can
talk about my own decline with a lightheartedness, it can be easier for
others to embrace and accept what I am sharing with them.

Most of my friends have had a positive response, offering support and willingness to learn along with me what this new reality
means to me and our relationships. Some friends have faded away.
One friend distanced himself as if this disease was contagious. He
also seemed to think that with this early diagnosis, I must already be
in the end stages of dementia. He, like many others, see neurocog-

nitive disease through a stereotypical lens—if you have cognitive issues, then you must be nonfunctional. When this attitude is present, people will speak around me rather than to me or raise their voice as if I were deaf, making assumptions about what I can and can't comprehend.

It can be exhausting to have these conversations, although most often I am very glad that I have taken the time to talk openly and honestly about this ignored issue. I know that it is only through recognizing the stigma that exists socially and personally that I can live fully in my own skin. Having cognitive changes is only one aspect of who I am, and this is true for all others facing this diagnosis. Lifting up and making this invisible issue visible can bring acceptance on a personal level and move us toward a cultural shift to a more loving and caring model of care and support.

MULTIDIMENSIONALITY

We are all more than a disease, illness, and our achievements, faults, and foibles. Bias and stigma ignore this truth. Our individual uniqueness cannot be completely erased, even as behaviors change, identities are forgotten, and memories are lost. The basic goodness of our humanity remains intact beyond our ability to express it overtly or control our behaviors. This is because we are multidimensional beings. There is more to us than just one aspect of who we are.

Mary was one example of this, though she would not have called herself multidimensional. In spite of her cognitive deficits, she continued to act as the matriarch of her family, enjoying visits from grand- and great-grand kids, even when she didn't know exactly who they were. Receiving Catholic Communion and reciting the Lord's Prayer continued to bring her peace until the end of her life. Even in the depth of her dementia, she would express care and concern for other residents at the skilled nursing facility. If she saw someone alone, she would make a point to go over to them and smile or offer her hand. Realizing this multidimensionality as a part of being human can help us develop confidence in our ability to meet future challenges. Calling on all parts of ourselves, especially our strengths, whatever they may be, can help us adapt to the changing shape of our lives.

I try to remember this about myself, when I feel stigmatized or embarrassed by my memory loss. A few months ago, a friend had an opening exhibition of his photographs. Frank and I attended along with many mutual friends we hadn't seen since the beginning of the COVID-19 pandemic in 2020. A woman I didn't recognize approached me with her arms outstretched and a warm and loving smile, reaching for my hands. As she took my hands, she offered me her name, clearly aware that I couldn't place her. This was a very kind gesture on her part, and appropriate since I had no idea who she was, and yet I felt embarrassed. I shrunk myself down in the crowd, watching the people around me instead of engaging. I needed time to take in what had just happened and my response to it. After a few minutes of quiet time in the middle of this lively event, I felt ready to step back into conversation with someone who seemed safe—in other words, someone I still recognized. Life has become a bit of a juggling act for me, especially at public events. I rely on certain strategies to help me maneuver through embarrassing situations like this, such as my ability to care for myself by allowing uncomfortable feelings to come up and gradually dissolve on their own. Since we are all multidimensional, this type of internal strength can help me balance those times when I feel lost in a conversation or don't recognize what should be a familiar face.

Multidimensionality encourages me to remain open to the multiple facets of others as well. I had several follow-up visits with the physician I described at the beginning of this chapter. During these interactions he was caring, personable, and patient. I still don't know why he had such a gruff disposition at our first encounter, but I am glad I had the opportunity to see this other part of who he is.

Being multidimensional creatures, each one of us can discover the aspects of ourselves we can call on when meeting new challenges. We can also remain open to the variety of features that may be revealed about someone else's nature. I realize that my way of coping now will change over time as my cognitive abilities change. I also trust that at the deepest level, the essence and very heart of being human— buddha nature—will continue to shine through, in the gaps between future anxieties, confusion, and forgetfulness.

JUST LIKE ME

Over a decade ago I had the honor of living at Gampo Abbey, a Western Buddhist monastery in Nova Scotia, Canada. This was the main residence of Pema Chödrön at the time and she was leading the community through a closed winter retreat. Gampo Abbey is a complex of buildings that started as a renovated farmhouse and barn that sits on a cliff overlooking the Gulf of St. Lawrence on Cape Breton Island. Its remote and naturally beautiful setting is a perfect place for contemplative study within a small community of like-minded people.

The Gampo Abbey community was a mix of lifelong monks and nuns, staff, and work-study residents. Residents who were lay practitioners had the opportunity to take temporary monastic vows while living at the Abbey to deepen their practice. Life at the Abbey blended silent reflection, meditation classes, dharma teachings, and daily work schedules. This gave everyone that lived there multiple opportunities to work with their own minds in an environment of practice and study. We all shared a commitment to develop our personal awareness, connecting at a deeper level with our basic goodness. This sounds like a peaceful setting, but in reality, Pema often described Gampo Abbey as a house of mirrors, where our worst tendencies could erupt against our will. This was considered good news, as unearthing these uncomfortable tendencies would then allow us to recognize and work with them.

As a part of the winter retreat Pema was leading that year, she gave us a new on-the-spot practice to work with as a group. We spent many hours in silence while living a communal life. This could lead to all sorts of opportunities to work with our thoughts, as there were few distractions. Speculation about what others were thinking when they brushed past you in the narrow hallways could become full-blown melodramas in your head during the hours of silence. In this pressure-cooker environment, Pema was asking us to consider how much alike we all are. This practice is called "Just Like Me."

The contemplation that goes along with this practice is that, just like me, all beings wish to be happy and free from suffering. This is a simple, easy-to-remember phrase that truly levels the playing field between yourself and others.

So each morning as we ate our breakfast in silence, I would look around the dining room thinking, "So-and-so over there, who maybe I'm not very fond of, is just like me." Looking at another table, "There is so-and-so who I think talks too much. Maybe, just like me, they wish to be happy and free of suffering." Adding the Just Like Me Practice into the self-reflective atmosphere of Gampo Abbey began to melt away some of these internal judgments about those around me and myself.

Tempers noticeably softened throughout the community. People began to slow down in the hallways and smile, making eye contact with each other instead of hurriedly brushing past. The Just Like Me Practice had ripple effects for the entire group. Eventually, as I have continued to use this practice over many years, it has shifted my worldview. I can be more patient and understanding when things don't go my way or I feel disempowered by someone's words or actions.

I know that there are many people who are trying to make sense of a new diagnosis and how to go forward into an uncertain future—just like me. Recognizing the interconnectivity of all who are facing this disease eases my sense of isolation so common for people living with a neurodegenerative disease. I feel less alone.

The Just Like Me Practice develops our ability to connect at a deeper level, beyond differences of opinion or personality. This can be of great benefit for anyone who is feeling stigmatized or alienated by others, and for all who are working toward liberating internal biases from their hearts and minds. Thinking of the phrase *just like me* helps me look past the stigma I encounter and invites me to try to connect at the heart level, even with those who may unknowingly act in a biased or impolite manner.

PRACTICE

Just Like Me Practice

Just Like Me is a simple practice for recognizing the universality of our human experience. By paying attention to those we encounter throughout the day and thinking to ourselves, "Just like me, this person wants to be happy and free from suffering," we connect with our own humanity and develop a sense of belonging and equanimity with others.

As an on-the-spot meditation, you can choose when you would like to try it out. In the beginning, I found that it was helpful to have a particular time that I was going to focus on it, such as a trip to the store or a lunch date with a friend.

Then anyone that I would meet and have a thought about, good or bad—"Her hair looks nice," "He's talking so loudly," or feeling annoyed by the person asking for money on the street corner—I would follow the thought with "Just like me, they wish to be happy and free from suffering."

Now that I'm familiar with the practice, I sometimes shorten it for brief interactions. When passing someone on the street, I think, "Just like me," as I make eye contact with them.

This is an experimental practice. You can change the wording and play with how and when you use it. If you find ways to incorporate it into your thoughts regularly, you may be surprised at how this softens your heart and opens your eyes a little wider to those around you.

5

~

The Golden Opportunity—
When Symptoms Arise

How can I regret
A future that was never promised
Or the past that I tried to store
    away on a dusty shelf?

Both—dissolve in the sunlight
Striking the oak floor
Where I stand to warm my cold feet.
—SHARON LUKERT

Last fall, Frank and I were raking up the leaves in our yard. It was a simple, routine moment for us as we slowly raked up the crunchy red maple leaves and talked about the garden. Frank asked a question about preparing the vegetable garden for the next year's planting. "Should we put the compost down now in the fall or wait until the spring?" We are used to making such day-to-day decisions together, and I tend to take the lead in the garden planning. This question wasn't rocket science or unusual, but my brain could not make sense of it.

I froze in the moment and couldn't think. The more I tried to figure it out, the more irritated and confused I felt. I kept raking, not looking up, as I tried to comprehend what was going on internally. Why couldn't I answer this? Frank asked again, with a quizzical look. Finally I shook my head and simply said, "I can't talk about this right now. Can we talk about it later?" and I walked away.

I don't think Frank noticed, but I was quite shaken. It was the first time I realized that my brain couldn't compute information in the way I'm used to. There was a strange visceral feeling that happened along with the confusion and irritation. I've come to call this a "neural shiver." I liken it to the sound of fingernails scratching a chalkboard, or being at a loud concert with flashing lights, in the middle of a crowd, and trying to recite a poem you learned in grade school. That's the type of sensory overload I felt when Frank asked me about composting the garden. It sent an actual shiver down my spine and raised goose bumps on my arms.

This was one of my early "Oh no" moments, a time of disorientation and inability to think clearly along with a sinking feeling in my gut and a racing heart. I wondered what this meant: "Is it a new normal for me? Am I progressing more quickly than expected? Is this the quicksand slide into dementia?" The shape of my life was changing. As I tried to make sense of it all, I needed time to integrate this new situation into my very being. It felt like a free fall without a parachute.

What I couldn't know in that moment was that this type of experience would come and go in inconsistent and unexpected ways rather than becoming a new solid reality, until my memory fails me completely.

UNPREDICTABLE AND ILLOGICAL

My doctor once told me that this disease is unpredictable and illogical. I have come to realize for myself that Alzheimer's disease is not a linear progression with a well-delineated path from normal cognition to dementia. Standing at the gateway of Alzheimer's is more of a slow slog through brambles in the darkness of a moonless night, then stepping into an open flowering field of sunshine, all leading slowly down a gradual path into the valley of dementia.

The changes begin subtly and sporadically, growing in significance over a long period of time. The odd thing for me is that there are times when my memory is quite clear, and I can help Frank find the car keys. Yet each time a symptom arises—a loved one's name forgotten, a familiar route suddenly alien—groundlessness occurs. In these moments of sudden disorientation, I must draw on deep reserves of self-compassion, curiosity, and openness in order to face the unpredictable and illogical nature of this disease.

GROUNDLESSNESS

Groundlessness is often described in Buddhism as a positive outcome of letting go and allowing the flow of life and uncertainty to freely move through you. In the beginning to work with groundlessness in meditation, it is often very uncomfortable. Groundlessness can be overwhelming. Many of the practices in Tibetan Buddhism are designed to introduce the practitioner slowly and methodically to letting go of attachments and resting in an open and fluid spaciousness. Through training, one can become more familiar with the felt sense of groundlessness. What may feel like an all-consuming catastrophe at the beginning can, over time, become more tolerable as the practitioner remains open to experiencing it. The purpose of staying with this feeling is to develop a sense of resilience, similar to the purpose of the Pause Practice, so that sudden changes are less disruptive.

The new experience of the neural shiver when I was raking leaves that fall day was confusing and concerning for me. It was difficult for me to apply the practices regarding groundlessness as I stood there with rake in hand. To the contrary, I wanted to push it away. It has taken time and effort to allow myself to rest and accept these times when I shiver and my mind is blank.

In Zen Buddhism there is a teaching that revolves around a phrase "don't-know mind." Resting in a state of not knowing means letting go of concepts and thoughts altogether and being open to whatever you are experiencing in that moment with curiosity. When I can remember this during a state of confusion or disorientation, I may still be confused, but I can relax with it. Then there is a little space to allow the confusion to just be and for me to allow that sense of groundlessness without being swallowed whole by it.

GOOD AND BAD BRAIN DAYS

These neural shivers and brain blips are not constants in my life but tend to ebb and flow in an unpredictable fashion. I have noticed a pattern of having some good days, with few cognitive issues, and bad days, when I feel like I am fumbling through a perceptual fog all day long.

On a good day, my brain seems to be firing on all cylinders and my energy seems as strong as ever. I may have a series of good days that can last a week or more. During these periods, I can doubt whether my diagnosis is accurate. Now I think of these times as a fleeting blessing to savor. However, if I try to do too much, a good day can easily slide into exhaustion and depletion.

On a bad brain day, I trip over words, forget what I was in the midst of doing, and can lose my way around the neighborhood. I've come to know some triggers that can set off a bad brain day, including stress of any kind, lack of sleep, or a sudden change of plans.

As symptoms seem to be slowly progressing, some of these issues seep into my everyday life just a little bit more, not just on those bad brain days. Becoming aware of these good and bad brain days can help me sort out when to dive into a full day of activity and when to take a break and try to relax. Though it can be frustrating to kick back and decrease my expectations for what I can accomplish on any given day, trying to develop more relaxation and time for rest each day seems to lessen the exhaustion and overall frustration of not being able to get as much done as I used to be capable of.

WHAT IS IT LIKE?

I believe it is important for people to understand what this experience can be like so that the understanding of the difference between normal forgetfulness with aging and mild cognitive impairment is more familiar. Each person with cognitive issues will have a different experience, so I can only speak about my symptoms. I am not used to speaking or writing about these issues openly, but I have decided that this is important to do to advance the conversation about cognitive decline to a deeper level.

When curious friends ask me to explain what MCI is like, I mention forgetting appointments or what day it is. But this doesn't tell the whole story of my changing reality. Here I will dive deeper into the idiosyncrasies of my particular changing brain cells. This is not written as a litany of complaints or to initiate a pity party. I have no reason to complain or seek sympathy; my only intention is to shine a light on what it is like to go through cognitive decline and to let those going through similar circumstances know they are not alone.

Memory Loss

I have forgotten a number of appointments, even with the aid of calendars, an iPhone, and a smartwatch with synchronized reminders. Because of the inconsistent nature of my memory now, I can't be sure if I am remembering a date and time correctly. As an example, I have missed or been late for so many haircut appointments that my hairstylist now sends me a personal text with her own reminder. Something she doesn't normally do, but I appreciate her friendly nudge to help me get there on time and on the right day.

A part of my missing appointments has to do with a change in my perception of time, as well as memory changes. This perceptual shift may not be listed as one of the ten early signs of Alzheimer's disease, but it is a common signal of mild cognitive impairment. It seems that my internal sense of time sometimes crumbles into a wadded-up piece of cellophane that is hard to decipher. Just the other day I had a Zoom appointment at 4:15 p.m. I was sure to prepare ahead of time and was sitting at my desk with computer open and ready by 4:00. Somehow I got distracted—I can't even say how—and before I knew it, it was already 4:20 and I hadn't signed on. This is confounding for me, as in my professional life I prided myself on my timeliness and ability to manage multiple meetings during any given day. Now there are times when I walk around chanting to myself, "This is Thursday, this is Thursday" over and over throughout the day, trying to make it stick, only to lose track of what I was planning to do on Thursday.

A few months after my initial diagnosis, I was meeting with some colleagues in the Spiritual Care Department where I used to work. I decided it was time for me to share my diagnosis with the team. I explained the situation and told them that I had become unreliable. Two of the three were surprised and expressed their well-wishes for my health; the third person was unusually quiet. I asked him what he was thinking. He said I had already told him this news two weeks earlier. We all had a good chuckle as my unreliability became very apparent in real time.

Lost Words

Another symptom of my changing cognition has been losing my vocabulary and trouble with finding words, such as the "marigold incident" mentioned in the first chapter. Frank has gotten very good at guessing and filling in the blanks for me when I get stuck. It is more difficult for me to keep up with a conversation if it includes several people or if someone is speaking quickly. I can't always follow the topic, and I just can't come up with the words I want very quickly, if at all. Thoughts I may want to share seem to disappear like rising smoke from a campfire. Most of this may not be apparent to others, but I am very aware of how I have stepped back from in-depth conversations at gatherings.

I can write with much more ease than I can speak. When I speak, the words are coming unfiltered through a short-circuited brain. With writing, the words are coming from my heart, slow and deliberate. Journaling and poetry became a means of expression for me as a teenager, and now in my later years, they are a welcome way for me to communicate once again. It helps that I can go back and correct mistakes or fill in the blanks; and I rely heavily on my handy assistant, "Madame Thesaurus," regularly.

Lost Items

Frank and I have a running joke about how many items I have lost. It started back in 2021 when I lost my eyeglasses for the first time. We searched the house, the yard, even our neighborhood walking route, but we couldn't find them. They showed up the following spring in the compost pile! Since then, I have lost two more pairs of glasses, a paring knife, a sweater, and a cutting board. None of these items have been found so far.

Trouble with Math, Numbers, and Analog Clocks

Another surprising impact of my cognitive decline has been struggling with math and numbers. I seem to have lost the ability to add and subtract easily in my head. Math used to be a strong skill for me, as I took precalculus classes in high school, calculated medication doses as a nurse, and routinely tended to my finances my entire adult life. Now, Frank has taken the lead financially. Although I remain engaged with paying the bills and maintaining the budget, I can no longer tend to these tasks alone. This lack of ability to calculate seems to be connected to my inconsistent ability to read an analog clock. Sometimes the hands and numbers on the clockface just don't make sense.

Lost Faces and Locations

Recognizing familiar faces and locations has also become unpredictable. In general, this has remained the exception so far; usually I know who is who. Several times I haven't recognized people I know well, like the time at the photo exhibition mentioned earlier. There have also been a number of times when I have looked around during a walk and I am not sure where I am, even in my neighborhood.

I do a mental dance throughout the day, every day—an invisible level of cognitive concern I don't speak about much with others. It seems that my brain has assigned different names for certain people and places. I have to mentally stop and correct myself before I say someone's name out loud. My sister-in-law, Kim, and I are very close, yet mentally, when I think of her, the name Rachel pops up. So far I have avoided calling her Rachel to her face, but I wonder how long I will be able to internally self-correct. This happens with a number of people I know well, stores where I shop regularly, and local street names. It is taxing on my energy and diminishes my self-confidence when I can't trust my brain to provide the right names for those I love and routine places in my life.

Many of my earlier vacations have been road trips. I would venture out alone for cross-country drives—just me, some music, and a road map. Now I have become poor with directions, even around town. It has taken a while for me to realize that I can't give reliable directions to others, even to get back to my house. I often point to the wrong intersection, say left instead of right, and am incorrect at least 85 percent of the time. I miss the role of being the navigator when Frank and I go places, as I often misinterpret Siri's instructions when telling Frank about the turns coming up ahead. Shifts in perceptions of time and space and a slower ability to process information have altered how I relate to the world around me.

Focus and Energy Shifts

Uncertainty creeps into my daily plans and decisions as it is hard to gauge how well my energy level will hold up. I asked about the symptom of increased tiredness during a course, Healthy Living with Mild Cognitive Impairment, offered by the Alzheimer's Association. When I brought up my concern, I learned that this is often an unspoken symptom for people with MCI. The facilitator explained that the brain is working much harder to complete the tasks that are normally routine. This depletes one's energy and can lead to tiredness and to becoming easily overwhelmed.

I often feel fine until suddenly I don't. As this is more common now, I try to plan ahead and have an escape plan in mind for large gatherings and public events. Sometimes taking a few extra minutes in the restroom or slipping into the background at a public event allows me some respite. Other times, I may choose to stay home if I anticipate the event would be too long or too loud.

Last spring I was a keynote speaker at a major fundraising event for the Wisconsin Alzheimer's Association. It was a large venue with hundreds in attendance, live music, and a silent auction near an open bar prior to the sit-down dinner. The staff thoughtfully set up a quiet room for those like me who would find this crowded and loud environment hard to manage. There I was able to rest for a while before joining the group for dinner and the presentations without feeling too wiped out.

Difficulty with distractions have also become an issue. If there is too much stimulation or I am trying to focus on something that I am having trouble understanding—say, a new problem with my computer—my patience wears thin easily. I can have a momentary meltdown as a neural shiver passes through my body and my brain goes offline. Frank now asks if I am ready for a question, to give me time to pause what I am doing, especially if I am cooking or raking leaves. This overload can also happen in busy places such as an airport or riding along a crowded highway.

The Jam Story

I forgot to mention one symptom that I just experienced this morning. I've become clumsy. I took a break from writing and went to the grocery store to get some basic items. As I was placing things on the cashier's conveyor belt, I knocked the jar of sugar-free strawberry jam against the side of the counter and it dropped to the floor, leaving a puddle of splintered glass and red jam.

When something like this happens, especially in public, my thoughts become scattered as I feel flustered and a little bit panicky. The cashier and customer behind me were very kind and patiently suggested I could pick up a replacement, but my hands were shaking and I couldn't imagine retrieving another jar of jam. I packed up my other groceries and hightailed it home.

Sometimes it seems as though these changes sneak up on me. I am going about my normal day, like today, and then there's this "Oh no" and the sinking feeling of disorientation takes over. A good day has just been turned upside down as the jar smashed to the floor and my confidence hit the ground.

It is the unpredictable nature of not knowing when my brain is functioning fully and when it is not that can be so disconcerting. All of the symptoms that I experience come and go in a way that can't be neatly mapped out on paper. Writing this section of the book has been both sobering and vulnerable for me. I hope that this can initiate open and honest conversations for those reading this book with cognitive changes; and curiosity and patience for those who are their care partners and loved ones.

THE ROLE OF JOURNALING

Journal writing has become an important tool for me to track and reflect upon new changes as they occur. Journaling about these cognitive changes allows me to feel a bit more in control. This also provides a chronological record of events and symptoms and a prompt for self-reflection, which has turned out to be very beneficial over time.

At first, journal writing was an attempt on my part to track my path toward dementia. Initially I had a sense of urgency, as it seemed to me that I was moving toward dementia quickly. I felt that I was running out of time. Now I realize this march toward dementia is a long, slow, uneven path, not a quick step dance. Yet it can seem like new challenges pop up often.

I found reviewing my journal to be a surprising and revealing exercise that I had not expected when I first began taking note of this process. One quiet day last winter when we were housebound by a snowstorm, I decided to read back through my journal. To my surprise, I read that I recognized the same symptom as if it were new and never before experienced, over and over.

Turning the pages back from January to September, I had written on three different occasions that I couldn't read an analog clock for the first time. Each time there was that "Oh no" moment, thinking this was a new symptom and a sign that my cognition was worsening. Each time, I had forgotten that this had happened before. This was an unexpected level of memory loss I had not been aware of.

There was some comic relief in this realization, like watching a set of clowns at the circus running circles around a miniature car, jumping in and out, all of them never quite making it into the car at the same time. I had to laugh at myself as my thoughts and memories jumped in and out of the metaphorical car of my brain. This helped me relax with the fact that there is only so much control I can have over these changes. Even with close scrutiny and monitoring, the new neural dance in my head is not something I can predict.

SELF-TALK

We all have an inner critic. For some of us, that inner critic can have a very harsh and loud voice that is overly judgmental and demanding. My meditation practice for the past thirty years has helped me lower the volume and soften the tone of my inner critic. But as I began to have more cognitive issues and meltdowns, the inner critic seemed to find its harsh voice once again, after all these years.

I remember a time recently when I was struggling to understand some instructions online. As I kept trying to push the right buttons and read through the process over and over, I became more confused and frustrated. Gritting my teeth and shaking my laptop, I shouted out, "Stupid! I'm just so stupid." I'm embarrassed to say that this adolescent outburst came out of my mouth so spontaneously, I wondered who even said it.

After a few minutes of heavy breathing and pacing the kitchen floor, I tried to calm down my heart rate and this angry internal voice. It was such a surprise and disappointment that my inner critic could still hold these hard words against me. I felt defeated.

I know that we may not have control over the circumstances of our lives, but we can have some control over how we respond to them. It is just as true that there are times when our worst selves come forward to greet us, uninvited. At that moment while pacing in the kitchen, all I could do was allow myself to feel the defeatedness of that defeat.

Where's the Golden Opportunity?

It is easier to apply my practices and feel kindhearted toward myself and others when things are going relatively well in my life. Accepting that my abilities are changing in a way that challenges my patience and self-compassion may not seem like a golden opportunity for connecting with and extending basic goodness. It is definitely uncomfortable and frustrating. Where is the gold among the muck and mire of defeat, self-deprecation, and frustration? Having to face some of my own inner demons provides me with the opportunity to know myself a little bit better and acknowledge all parts of myself that I may not have paid attention to otherwise.

Skills for caring for myself have become more important to cultivate now. I look to provide myself with opportunities for rest and relaxation without a sense of guilt for tasks left undone. Taking a short hike in our neighborhood or along the bluffs of the Mississippi River can soothe the inner critic as I connect with the natural world that surrounds and supports me. Taking a hot bath can calm my nerves and help me sleep better. Listening to music and dancing in the kitchen bring me joy. Beyond these self-care measures, there is also an advantage to making friends with these so-called negative personality traits.

Acceptance can be an overused concept in psychological circles. I realized this as a hospice chaplain as I witnessed patients who considered the stages of dying proposed by Elisabeth Kübler-Ross to be a singular and linear process. They and their care partners would struggle trying to reach the golden ring of acceptance, where they thought they could rest in the warm light of peace until they died. What I learned at the bedside was that the emotional process of dying was shaped more like the tides, in constant motion, rather than a straight line. Acceptance would come and go, then circle around again along with a plethora of other feelings and thoughts. There was no specific end point where someone could reach the precipice of acceptance and remain there till their last breath.

Acceptance is sometimes claimed to be an oasis of grace and rest for those with chronic disorders. I think the same applies for those with chronic illness as it does in the dying process; there is no static end point. Acceptance is likely to ebb and flow just like all of our thoughts and emotions. Yet there is some benefit in developing a level of acceptance of our changing selves. This acceptance may not look like a final stage of unending joy, but it can be an honest state of openness to all the parts of ourselves, including our frustration and loving-kindness toward ourselves and others.

The golden opportunity lies in recognizing that these new sensations, thoughts, and feelings are a part of the new shape of our life. We can befriend the parts of ourselves that may seem alien and distasteful—the fear, discouragement, confusion, loss, and failure. As I have become more familiar with them, they are more manageable. These unwanted feelings continue to rise up in me, but they are no longer strangers.

Times when self-reproach is strong, it can be difficult to remember that we all hold within us the seeds of natural goodness. Tapping into this source of compassion, love, and joy can help transform any challenging situation into an opportunity to experience a deeper connection within ourselves and with others. This includes our mistakes and missteps born of our diminishing brain cells.

Loving-kindness is the ground within the groundlessness of disorientation and confusion. We can develop kindness and acceptance, to forgive ourselves when we make mistakes and to love the parts of ourselves we want to push away. This is a long-term practice because our internal biases toward ourselves don't change easily. But the effort is well worth it when we can embrace who we are now, with all our foibles and fumbles.

My meditation teachers provided wise advice that helped me recognize these frightening experiences and the fear itself as opportunities to embrace reality as it is. Learning to accept moments of disorientation as opportunities to connect at a deeper level with myself allows these new symptoms to break my heart open rather than shutting me down. Loving-kindness toward ourselves in order to work with our internal narratives and our shifting emotional landscape can bring us a sense of ground under our feet in the midst of unpredictable and illogical change. The Handshake Practice is a straightforward way to meet our inner demons with love, openhearted acceptance, and curiosity.

❧

GUIDED MEDITATION

The Handshake Practice

The Handshake Practice was introduced by Tsoknyi Rinpoche, a well-known Tibetan Buddhist teacher. Pema learned this technique from Tsoknyi Rinpoche and has been passing it on to her students and followers as a step toward developing loving-kindness toward all parts of ourselves.

This simplified version of the Handshake Practice is a way to begin to accept the parts of ourselves that we would prefer to ignore or reject. If you are interested in further instruction, see the resources at the back of the book.

Begin by taking a few slow, deep breaths, closing your eyes and relaxing into your body.

Now bring to mind a feeling that you consider negative, one that haunts you. This may be jealousy, irritation, anger, or sadness. This feeling is one that is uncomfortable for you, yet it seems to follow you around. Tsoknyi Rinpoche calls this feeling "the beautiful monster." It is beautiful because it is a part of you. It is a monster because you don't like it; you try to push it away or ignore it.

Now imagine that one of your hands is this feeling. Your hand represents this beautiful monster in a fist—ready to fight, to jump up at any moment.

Your other hand is your sense of loving-kindness. This hand represents your ability to be open, gentle, and kind to yourself and others.

It is open and soft. It doesn't try to change anything, to push away or ignore the beautiful monster of your other hand.

Now with one hand in the tight fist of jealousy, or whatever feeling you are resisting, place the open hand of kindness on top of it and gently, softly hold that beautiful monster hand steady.

Perhaps this hand begins to stroke the beautiful monster. Perhaps just resting softly as the monster hand resists is all that you can do. The key is in the attitude of the kindness hand—letting the beautiful monster know it's supported and allowed to feel what it's feeling without judgment.

Once this practice becomes familiar to you, it can become an easy reminder at times when those feelings come up in your life. When you are in the grocery store and become irritated with the person in line ahead of you, gently stroke your fist with your other hand, softening and opening to your irritation without needing to act on it or suppress it.

This is how we develop loving-kindness toward all the multitudes of feelings and thoughts we have that are all a part of who we are—the good, the bad, and the ugly. Every moment, every feeling becomes a golden opportunity to embrace every part of who we are. This builds inner strength and openness to the beauty of life as it is, including the monsters, afflictions, and all.

6

Testing, Diagnosis, and Studies—Oh My!

Within the chilled October breeze
A first frost drifts across the sleeping garden.
Winter heaves awake slowly,
With a raspy voice the soil whispers, waiting.

This is the between time.
After the first flush of diagnosis,
Before the impending sunset of dementia.
Just now—waiting.

Both wonderment and fearful trepidation—
Hold on tight.
Ice forms around the edges,
A last leaf sways heavy with snow—waiting.

For strength and comfort, I breathe in—
Deeply bitter-cold air, exhilarating and piercing.

This is the in-between time.

Waiting—just now—waiting.

—SHARON LUKERT

It is a chilly November afternoon, and I am sitting in the waiting room of the neuroscience department—again. The neurocognitive testing and visit with the neuropsychologist to monitor my cognition has become as much a part of my annual medical care as a blood pressure check and routine lab tests. I am filled with anxious anticipation and remind myself to breathe slow and deep to calm my nerves. Frank is sitting next to me and is handed the same questionnaire as the first visit to update his observations of my abilities and how his role as a "caregiver" is affecting him.

Entering the realm of the Western medical systems for testing and diagnosis, or to participate in research, can feel like landing in a foreign country. The language and customs can be unfamiliar, even if you are accustomed to them. I have worked most of my adult life within health care and was raised in a household where my mother's stories about her work as a nurse were part of our regular dinner conversations, so I feel more at home within the medical system than most. But entering as a patient with cognitive issues is a very different experience compared to working as a provider or caregiver. It has been very confusing and frustrating at times. As one friend expressed, it can become a full-time job just to keep up with appointments and medical recommendations.

It could be easy for me to get lost in an account of the medical and technical details. However, I realize that whatever I write today regarding medical treatments and breakthroughs in research will be out of date by the time you read these words. But how we cope with the demands, decisions, and the confusing systems when seeking health care can be an unchanging factor within our control. I am most interested and curious about how meditation and the practices of mindfulness and loving-kindness for yourself and others can be supportive when entering the territory of a health-care system.

At first I felt alone in this journey, until I met several contemporary companions who are going through similar challenges. Some of these companions are friends who have shared their diagnosis of mild cognitive impairment with me. Some I have met through the Alzheimer's Association classes and support groups for people with MCI. In order to broaden my understanding regarding the experience of testing and receiving a diagnosis beyond my singular experience, I asked a few of them if they would be willing to share their stories. Their voices and mine combine to provide a broader glimpse into how the medical world intersects with the lives of those they serve with cognitive issues.

Sheri Lowe is a retired therapist who became interested in meditation before it was popular and has practiced meditation for more than two decades. She became a meditation instructor based on Mindfulness-Based Stress Reduction (MBSR) developed by the scientist and meditation teacher Jon Kabat-Zinn. As a therapist, she and a colleague incorporated meditation into a recovery program for people with addictions. She led these weekly groups for several years prior to retiring. Sheri was diagnosed with early onset dementia, meaning her symptoms began at a relatively young age. She is in the beginning stages of the disease. I met her through a Healthy Living with Mild Cognitive Impairment online course, where she led the group through a guided meditation. When I approached her about an interview for this book, she was excited to share her voice.

Sid* is a friend who lives in La Crosse, Wisconsin, my hometown. We first met in 2016 through mutual friends and a common interest in meditation. Sid was diagnosed with mild cognitive impairment more than four years ago. He is a retired social worker and has been meditating for many years. When I told him I was writing this book, he was very happy to sit down with me and share his journey in order to shed more light on the personal experience of being tested, receiving a diagnosis, and living with MCI.

TESTING

I don't know anyone who enjoys the process of testing, especially the in-depth neurocognitive testing that can take anywhere from one and a half to three hours. It can feel demeaning to struggle with repeating a series of words or being timed as you draw lines between numbers and letters. Being asked to complete math problems in my head is my least favorite part of the test. I excelled in math and science in high school, but rudimentary math skills are difficult now. When I asked Sid what testing was like for him, he said, "Scary. They tell you a story like, 'Jane and Dick go to the grocery store and buy celery, lettuce . . .' and so on. Then they come back to it like twenty minutes later and ask you what you remember about the story. That was hard."

As we talked about the method of neurocognitive testing, Sheri said, "My experience was not very good." She described how she felt during the initial test: "I didn't want to be there. I wanted to leave. I just kind of shut down as the neuropsychologist seemed bored and kind of angry with me." That experience felt so demeaning, it still bothers her years later.

While waiting to see Dr. Prichett, I overheard a man complain to his wife that he just doesn't want to go through the tests anymore. It felt like too much for him. I am sure some of you can relate. It can be exhausting. I often have a headache by the time the testing is finished. Sid shared with me that by the last half hour of the test, he wasn't able to concentrate any longer.

The tests are not perfect. Testing is done in a sterile environment, as opposed to our day-to-day experiences of using memory and other cognitive skills. I tend to be good at test taking. Back in high school, a million years ago, I wasn't the smartest person in my class, but I did well on the SATs. For some reason, taking a test focuses my mind. Many people have the opposite response; their mind goes blank under the pressure of taking any form of a test. Yet, at this time, the neuropsychology tests are one of the most accessible and predictable ways to detect early memory changes that are greater than normal.

Sequential testing, which compares your previous test scores to your current one, is the best way of identifying early changes. This means going through the process of testing on a regular basis, like a lab test for your cholesterol levels every few years. Thinking ahead to his upcoming testing session, Sid told me that he is still scared to be tested because he knows he is not going to like the outcome. He added, "It is my meditation practice that helps me through the most. It may not stop the MCI from getting worse, but it helps to keep me calm."

As I sit in the waiting room before this round of testing begins, I breathe slow and deep and wiggle my toes to remain grounded. I remind myself that I am more than just a score on a test or a diagnosis marked on my chart. My sequential testing has shown a steady and significant decline. Even though the results are still in the normal range, they are much lower than they were two years ago, which were lower than they were two years before that. I have lost ground in the categories of memory and my ability to retain new learning.

This was not a surprise to Frank or me as word finding and short-term memory have been more of a struggle lately. From my perspective, the true confirmation of my declining abilities was during a visit with my now six-year-old granddaughter, Scarlett. We were playing a game of "school" where she was the teacher and I was her student. She grew impatient with me as I wasn't able to answer a math problem correctly or repeat a story back to her properly. My math and memory skills had dropped below her kindergarten level of learning. Now that was a humbling experience. I had to breathe in my feelings of defeat while also allowing space in my heart to accept who I am today. It is in moments like these, when my cognition dissolves during what would normally be an easy exchange, that I realize how much my brain is changing. That has a stronger impact on me than any test result written in my chart ever could have.

The Privilege of Testing

Although the testing is rigorous and tiring, I realize it is also a privilege to be able to access these services so easily. Not everyone has this advantage. If I find it difficult to maneuver through the health-care and insurance systems, I imagine those without a background in this area or an advocate at their side might find it close to impossible. Not everyone has insurance that will cover the additional costs for the extensive testing required, or they may not be readily referred to a neuropsychiatrist by their primary care provider, if there is not such a specialist in their area. All of these obstacles mean that the testing and diagnostic process is not equitable due to economic, geographic, and cultural differences.

I know several friends who suspect they have cognitive changes beyond the norm but are reluctant to be tested. Often people mention the fact that there is no cure for Alzheimer's disease and related dementias as a reason to avoid testing. This, however, is based on a misunderstanding. There are actions one can take to improve your cognition, even if you do have Alzheimer's disease, and there are treatable causes for cognitive impairment that are reversible. Going through the testing process can help you take charge of factors that can enhance your memory and slow down progression, or it could lead to addressing an underlying issue that may be the primary cause for memory loss.

Even though the testing process can be challenging, it has also brought me a new sense of purpose and meaning. As a lifelong learner, I believe that knowledge is power. Understanding my condition provides me with a sense of control and autonomy. I view gaining an understanding about my health as a part of my Buddhist practice. Buddhist philosophy and practices are premised on the importance of becoming familiar with ourselves, which then extends into a clearer understanding of others and the world we live in. This clear seeing of ourselves and others includes accepting things as they are, not how we wish them to be. This is not a passive acceptance of hopelessness and helplessness but rather an openness and curiosity that can lead to understanding, compassion, and positive actions.

DIAGNOSIS

As you may imagine or you have lived through yourself, hearing that you have a neurocognitive issue can feel shocking and even devastating. How the message is delivered can vary widely and can have a strong impact on how you take in this news. I mentioned earlier my sense of shock when I was first told I have mild cognitive impairment. Sid said when he was first diagnosed that he just didn't believe it. He questioned the doctor as he thought there had been some kind of mistake.

For Sheri, the doctor was abrupt and dismissive. She remembers it as a horrible experience. The neurologist told her there was nothing they could do for her and she should go home and get her affairs in order. "I came home and sat in a chair, waiting to die. They took all hope away from me."

I believe the phrase "There is nothing we can do for you" should be banished from a health-care provider's vocabulary. Of course, what they mean is that there are no medical treatments at this time for Alzheimer's disease and related dementias, but there are things that can be done. You and your health-care provider can address factors that contribute to symptoms and, of course, your health-care team can evaluate and treat other causes for cognitive decline, such as certain medications, sleep apnea, or some blood deficiencies. An alternative message could be something like, "I am so glad you were willing to come in and be tested as there's lots we can explore together." A person can cope, manage, and even thrive while living with cognitive decline.

I have been fortunate that most of my encounters have been with caring, sensitive, and educated health-care providers. I was offered educational material about MCI at the time I was diagnosed and was referred to the local agency on aging to find resources and support. My hope is that more health-care providers and people working in health care in general will be trained in the appropriate information regarding cognitive decline and find compassionate and informed ways to deliver difficult news.

Sheri is using her challenging experience with testing and receiving her diagnosis to advise medical and speech therapy students about best practices for communicating with someone with dementia. This was new territory for Sheri: "I used to be scared to speak in public, but I don't have that fear anymore because they all know I have dementia, so if I can put a sentence together, they think it's wonderful!" She has discovered a new sense of purpose rising up from her diagnosis, and she is helping to bring a new awareness and sensitivity to the next generation of health-care providers.

What Does the Diagnosis Mean?

Mild cognitive impairment is not actually a disease. It is a syndrome or group of symptoms that can indicate an underlying condition or disease. This is also true of dementia, which is defined as a progressive loss of cognitive and other functions that interferes with activities of daily living. A diagnosis of these disorders does not shed light on what is causing the symptoms, and there can be multiple causes.

The difference between MCI and dementia is based on the person's ability to function on a day-to-day basis. I used to fear the time when my cognitive abilities would fall into the category of dementia. Now I realize that dementia is a human-made marker that delineates another shift on this continuum. The lived experience does not change in the same way as it may be described in a pamphlet or online. You don't move from stage 1 to stage 2 in a clear, linear fashion like driving from point A to point B. I like to think of the terms *mild cognitive impairment* and *dementia* as markers along a continuum from a normal aging process through to the other end of the spectrum of terminal end-stage neurodegenerative disease. Sheri captured the true feel of living with early dementia well when she described how she wished doctors would talk about a diagnosis with their patients: "They could say something like, 'I'm sorry to tell you this is dementia, but you can still be productive and still have joy. You're the same person today as you were yesterday before you knew this. Life goes on, you continue to be you, even in the midst of changing brain cells and memory loss.'"

Once it is established that someone has MCI or early dementia, the attention of the health-care team turns toward finding the cause. An accurate diagnosis of a neurological disorder is difficult to attain for many reasons. It is hard to study the brain and even more difficult to pinpoint what may be causing a person's symptoms as there can be so many contributing factors. There are a number of different neurological diseases beyond Alzheimer's disease, and it is possible to have several neurodegenerative processes simultaneously. Some research is currently focusing on more specific diagnostic tools.

The way cognitive diseases are being diagnosed is transforming as a result of recent discoveries in research. In the past, a clinical diagnosis of Alzheimer's disease was based on *ruling out* other causes. Now, with the new tests available such as PET scans, lumbar punctures, and blood tests to detect amyloid protein levels, Alzheimer's disease can be *ruled in* based on these findings. However, since there can be more than one brain disorder present at a time, this may only be a part of the story.

Misdiagnosis

The world of neuroscience has expanded the knowledge and understanding of neurocognitive disease exponentially in recent decades. And yet so much is still unknown. It often remains a waiting game for the specific disease or diseases to become evident as symptoms progress. It is not uncommon for neurological disease to be misdiagnosed.

It can be frightening to know that things are changing and not know why. Sheri said she noticed two to three years before her diagnosis that things were not right. "I started to forget what I was saying as I was speaking and mixing up people's names in the group. I felt they (her clients) deserved more and that something was wrong with me." Although it has been determined that she has dementia, the exact cause is still unknown.

I know one man who suffered from debilitating dizziness for several years before being properly diagnosed. Another told me she had symptoms for five years before finding out she has Parkinson's disease. I had visual changes along with cognitive changes, so it was suspected I had posterior cortical atrophy, an aggressive form of Alzheimer's disease that causes severe visual disturbances and a shortened life span. Only through hours of online searching and a bit of luck did I find the right specialist, a neuro-ophthalmologist, who ruled out this diagnosis and correctly recognized that I had an aggressive form of glaucoma unrelated to my cognitive issues.

From hearing these stories and my own experience, it is clear that our multidimensional nature is complex on every level, not only emotionally and spiritually but also physically. The elaborate and intricately connected makeup of the human body, especially the brain, continues to hold its own mysteries.

It takes patience to wade through the process of diagnosis, and as I mentioned, not all of these tests are available to everyone. Often, diagnosis of the underlying disease becomes apparent over time. The difficulty can be in the waiting. With all my years of meditation practice, I am still a rather impatient person. Waiting and developing patience around this process continues to be an opportunity for me to challenge my own edginess and anxiety and apply my meditative practices.

Benefits of an Early Diagnosis

I have found this early diagnosis has opened up deeper conversations with my family and some of my friends about future planning. It has also changed how I set priorities for living my best life now as well as in the years to come. Knowing I have MCI and will likely progress into dementia based on my elevated amyloid levels has given me a new sense of purpose. I want to deepen my understanding of this disease for myself and the millions of others who are also affected, just like me.

Most importantly for me, I have come to take this on as an adventure, to learn how I can apply my meditation practice with a sense of joy and acceptance to a life with cognitive decline, shattering the image of dementia as a dire and formidable enemy.

CLINICAL STUDIES

Once I realized that my mild cognitive impairment could be a preclinical step toward Alzheimer's disease, I began to look into clinical studies. This began as an altruistic attempt to find meaning and purpose in my new situation. If this illness was going to progress, then I wanted to find a way to use it to help others.

Finding the appropriate clinical study, however, was not easy. I began my search on the Alzheimer's Association website but had difficulty maneuvering through it. Once I had chosen a few studies to apply for, I sent out the email request forms. Often I did not receive a response. It took perseverance and patience to find a suitable study.

I learned that not all clinical studies are alike. It is important to consider the time needed to participate, including any travel necessary and exactly how the study is set up. Does the study require just a few sequential visits or monthly visits over a long period of time or is it a longitudinal study with annual visits required? Do they share your test results with you? And if so, do they assist you to find any necessary follow-up? A clinical study and a clinical trial are not the same. A study is data collection in order to better understand the neurodegenerative process. In a trial, the researchers are studying a potential treatment for effectiveness. The information can be a lot to weed through. Having a partner or friend who can help decipher the material can be very helpful.

Through trial and error I found a longitudinal study that is fairly close to home and only requires one or two visits a year, which is something Frank and I can commit to. This particular clinical study includes an annual visit so they can study any possible progression with neurological testing and blood tests. I also participate by having an MRI, lumbar puncture, and PET scans every few years.

Being active in clinical studies became a way for me to use my cognitive decline in a positive way with the hope of enhancing the lives of others, now and into the future. It also allowed me to learn more about my own illness. Volunteering to participate in a clinical trial or study is an act of kindness and generosity. This kind of research is an important part of changing the course of the understanding and treatment for Alzheimer's disease and related dementias in the future.

Participating in a clinical study or trial is one way that a person can find a sense of agency in the midst of what seems like a senseless illness. It isn't for everyone, but it can be rewarding to know that in one small way, you are contributing to the well-being of future generations of patients with cognitive issues.

FINDING SUPPORT AND RESOURCES

After I was diagnosed and the initial shock wore off, the natural next step for me was to search for more information. In the age of the internet, so much information is readily at hand. Sometimes this is very helpful. However, I would often get snared into surfing for the same information over and over. This occurred mainly in the middle of a sleepless night when worry would take over my thoughts. I realized that these midnight web-surfing sprees were generated by anxiety and feeling a loss of control. These binges were not really helpful to my overall well-being. Yet it was hard to resist this hunt for outside validation of my experience, even though I knew it just fed my fears. There was little online or in the books I read about mild cognitive impairment that was satisfying. Over time I realized that the answers I was looking for were about the lived experience of cognitive changes. This can only be found through connecting with others who are living with similar issues.

About six months after my initial diagnosis, Frank and I made an appointment with a dementia care specialist at our local Aging and Disability Resource Center, which is the statewide agency on aging in Wisconsin. We left the meeting with a portfolio filled with resources, information, and a sense of connection and hope. The comradery I eventually found through statewide support groups sponsored by the Alzheimer's Association and the educational opportunities provided by the Alzheimer's Disease Research Center at the University of Wisconsin–Madison have given me a new sense of community and belonging.

At the same time, taking in information about Alzheimer's disease and MCI can be challenging and difficult to digest. This is another time when gentleness is needed to avoid becoming overwhelmed by the amount of material available on the web and in books. My yoga instructor reminds her students to balance the inhalation and the exhalation breaths during our poses. This applies to taking in new information as well. When you are inhaling new material about potential future health issues, it is important to also let go and exhale with gentleness, giving yourself a break. There is no need to try to take it in all at once. Better to pace yourself, to pick and choose what is most helpful for you at any given time.

Support Groups

Sheri lost all hope and thought her life was over after her diagnosis. It wasn't until she was referred to an online support group for people with early dementia that she realized life goes on. She eagerly shared with me, "When I joined my first group, I was still feeling hopeless. Then I saw all these people laughing and talking about what they've been up to, and I thought, 'Well, I can do this too.'" Her group was virtual due to the pandemic, and it continues to be online. This has allowed the members to remain connected even after some of them moved away to be closer to family. Sheri said one of the advantages of these groups is they can just be themselves. It's okay if they can't find the right words or they forget what they were saying.

I have found the same to be true for me as well. My online support group helped me learn how to cope with situations when I felt overstimulated. This was particularly helpful as I prepared to travel to my daughter's home for the holidays. Planning some downtime during the day assisted me to be more present with my granddaughter. Sid and I share the desire for a local in-person support group. We may have to start one on our own as there are local groups for people with dementia but none for those of us with MCI.

Although there is no local group, Sid found his circle of friends to be supportive. He has kept himself active with friends, a local meditation group, and other activities such as tai chi and an ongoing men's support group.

There is a lot of power in a group. There is the collective wisdom, the support and empathy generated by helping each other out, and it can break the sense of isolation. It is a place where you can also share your skills and strengths. Sheri leads one of her groups in meditation each meeting. Several of the participants have now started meditating on their own.

Other Resources

One of the suggestions to prevent or stall cognitive decline is to engage in stimulating activities. One doctor said to me recently that the best thing I can do right now is to keep my brain as healthy as possible. This may not stop the process of neurodegeneration, but it may slow it down. I remain committed to living the best life I can for as long as I can, so I take his words seriously.

Once you connect with the resources in your area or online, you will find there are multiple ways to engage your mind and body in order to maintain your brain's health. This has become a new pursuit and another layer of motivation for me to watch my diet, continue to exercise, and remain as socially active as I can. For Sheri, Sid, and me, it has also strengthened our commitment to our meditation practice for ongoing emotional and spiritual support.

FORMAL MEDITATION

> We don't sit in meditation to become good meditators.
> We sit in meditation so that we'll be more awake in our
> lives.
> —PEMA CHÖDRÖN, *When Things Fall Apart:*
>   *Heart Advice for Difficult Times*[12]

I have been so happy to find Sheri and Sid, fellow meditators who also share a common thread of cognitive decline. Although we practice different forms of meditation, each of us has had a formal meditation practice for decades. This has provided a strong foundation that we rely on in a variety of ways. This same foundation is also available for those who are new to meditation who may wish to establish a new tool for enhancing their awareness and ability to work with their emotions and increase their appreciation and enjoyment of their lives just as they are right now.

There are many forms of meditation and just as many benefits from meditating regularly. Sheri uses meditation to help her stay in the present moment and work with anxiety. Sid says meditation has allowed him to meet his cognitive changes with lightness, humor, and a sense of acceptance. I have found my meditation practice allows me to let the emotional responses of frustration, anxiety, and sadness come and go, like the waves of the ocean lapping up onto the shore and receding again into the open waters. This kind of experience can be accessed even if you are new to meditation.

Why Begin Meditation Now?

There has been some research on the effects of meditation on cognitive decline. The results have been very promising. Studies have shown there are measurable positive changes in the brain structure after an eight-week course of nonsectarian meditation.[13] The studies differed somewhat in the form of meditation, though the most prominent form of practice focused on the breath for about fifteen minutes a day. All of the studies suggested more robust research was needed and offered hope that meditation is one way to slow the progression for early cognitive decline, and it is simple and easily accessible. Of course this is not a cure but one more method of increasing brain health daily, like eating those blueberries, which are highly recommended because of their antioxidant capacity.

You don't need to be Buddhist to meditate. In 1979, Jon Kabat-Zinn created Mindfulness-Based Stress Reduction, a mindfulness meditation program that introduced meditation for pain relief to the medical world. Other programs have followed, and there are many options to discover the approach that you are most comfortable with.

I have introduced you to a variety of on-the-spot practices in previous chapters. They are all based on formal meditation. In this chapter I introduce you to a simple formal meditation that you can incorporate into your daily life, beginning with just a few minutes a day. When practicing in this way, it can become easier to use the on-the-spot practices during your daily activities. You may find this time of sitting on a cushion or chair can become a quiet daily refuge you look forward to.

Awareness and Thoughts

Surprise is often the first response to sitting quietly and allowing your thoughts to come and go. You may become aware of how busy your thoughts are for the first time. You may also begin to touch a deeper sense of calm that is attainable by everyone. If you develop a routine of sitting, you will discover that the point is not to get rid of thoughts—no thought is intrinsically bad. I like to consider thoughts as a function of our brain, just like breathing is a function of our lungs. Our lungs keep breathing without us focusing on the breath. Our brain continues to produce thoughts even when we don't focus on them. Watching how a thought comes and goes can be soothing and can quiet the mind and body. We are often so caught up in our thinking that our other senses are ignored. By placing our awareness gently on our breath instead of our thoughts, we allow ourselves to be free from distraction for at least a few seconds at a time.

This doesn't mean that you won't get lost in thought. That still happens to me all the time. But I have come to trust that I will become aware of being lost at some point, then I bring my attention back to the breath without judgment or fanfare. I like to think of it as a flow from being aware of my breath to chasing a thought and back again. What has changed for me over the years is that when I recognize I have gone down a rabbit hole, chasing one thought into another, returning my awareness back to the breath is softer now. There is no need to force it; just allow your awareness to come back to the breath once you realize that you have been caught up in a train of thoughts.

CALM-ABIDING MEDITATION

Calm-abiding meditation was the first meditation technique I was introduced to and continues to be the foundation of my formal meditation practice. There are many different meditation techniques. You may be familiar with another form that is just as effective. It is more a matter of personal choice and what method you are familiar with. Most meditations focus on posture, a focal point, and how to work with your thoughts. In the Calm-Abiding Meditation, the focal point is your breath. This makes it very versatile, as your breathing is always available. If you are a beginner to meditation, it can be helpful to receive meditation instruction in person or find instructions online.

You don't need any fancy equipment to meditate. It can be helpful to have a quiet space, a chair or cushion to sit on, and a timer so you don't have to watch the clock. That is all you need, along with some motivation to practice this ancient art of getting to know your own mind with openness and curiosity.

~

GUIDED MEDITATION
Calm-Abiding Meditation

Start by sitting up tall in a comfortable position. If you are in a chair, your feet should be flat on the floor and your back should be straight, not leaning back against the chair. If you are sitting on a cushion, have your legs crossed, keeping your knees lower than your hips. If they are higher, you may need a higher cushion to sit on to be comfortable.

Your posture should be upright yet relaxed. Think of having a strong back without straining and with relaxed shoulders. Your front should be relaxed and open, not holding your belly in tight. You can rest your hands on your thighs or knees. Your chin is slightly tucked in and your lips are slightly parted. You can meditate with your eyes open or closed. If they are open, your gaze should be slightly lowered, about 45 degrees, and your focus is soft, so you are not straining to look at anything. If your eyes are closed and you begin to feel sleepy, try meditating with your eyes open.

The focus of this meditation is on the breath. The instructions are to follow your breath in a relaxed way. Pay attention to your breathing as you breathe in. Where do you feel it? Perhaps in your nose or chest. As you breathe out, allow your attention to go out with the breath as well.

When thoughts arise, which they naturally will, label them "thinking" and bring your attention back to the breath. Use a light touch, like a feather touching a soap bubble. It's important not to use a sledgehammer approach. Remember that the intention is to allow the thoughts to come and go, not to stop the process of thinking.

These instructions sound simple, which they are, though it can take some practice to feel familiar. Starting with short sessions and building up to longer ones can be helpful. Having someone you can talk to about your practice can be an invaluable support as well.

7

Living with Grace amid Paradox and Unpredictability

As human beings, not only do we seek resolution, but we also feel that we deserve resolution. However, not only do we not deserve resolution, we suffer from resolution. We don't deserve resolution; we deserve something better than that. We deserve our birthright, which is the middle way, an open state of mind that can relax with paradox and ambiguity.

—PEMA CHÖDRÖN, *When Things Fall Apart: Heart Advice for Difficult Times*

Paradox and uncertainty are a part of life. We can't escape the inconsistent and contradictory nature of how our lives and the lives of others intertwine and affect each other. Our health or the health of our loved ones can change without warning. The environment continually shifts, impacting how and where we live. With more extreme weather systems, even the seasons we have counted on for centuries are more unpredictable.

There are also paradoxes and internal contradictions within our-selves. Often I find myself reaching for yet one more chocolate while at the same time considering ways to improve my diet. This is the sort of inconsistency that comes along with being human. Paradox and uncertainty can undermine our wish for an easy and straight-forward life. It can be helpful to remember that life is full of such cognitive dissonances; they are inescapable and a part of our mul-tidimensional nature. As Pema Chödrön suggests, perhaps relaxing with this ambiguity would serve us better than striving for the illu-sion of a perfect life.

Having a sense of control while circumstances are continually changing in ways we have no actual control over is one expression of the paradoxical and uncertain nature of being alive. Knowing that we will die and not knowing when or how poses the ultimate mys-tery we each live with daily. Having this knowledge, consciously or unconsciously, influences our daily choices as we weigh the risks and benefits of our actions. Our mundane habits of watching the weather for impending storms and carefully looking both ways before cross-ing the street are based on our desire to be safe from harm and stave off death as long as possible. This is a very basic level of survival that all animals, including us, use to thrive in a world full of ambiguous causes and conditions.

UNEXPECTED CAREGIVING

The year 2023 was particularly trying and complicated for me and my entire family. I found myself facing a greater challenge than I could have ever anticipated as my family turned to me to take charge during a period of crisis and loss. My sister, Janet, became seriously ill in February and consequently died five months later on June 17, 2023.

Though the time span from the beginning of her illness to her demise was just five months, each day was filled with unpredictability, anxiety, and an overwhelming sense of helplessness. Of course, we had no idea how her path was going to unfold while we were going through it. This upended the homeostasis of the family. Our family looked to Frank and me for guidance and support and to carry the load of managing finances, legal issues, logistics, and caring for the physical and emotional needs for my sister, her husband, Joe—who also has cognitive issues rendering him unable to manage legalities or finances—and my ninety-three-year-old mother. This set us all into a chaotic state filled with grief and despair.

As a chaplain, I have accompanied many families through similar situations. However, that was not enough training to meet these new needs of my family without it taking a toll on my well-being. While I was struggling to keep my own calendar straight, I became responsible for tracking appointments for Janet, Joe, and my mom. I helped Janet with her showers and oversaw her medications during the month she was able to be at home between the hospital stay and her eventual move to a skilled nursing facility. Janet got upset when I would have trouble filling her weekly pill boxes. Although I tried my best to keep things afloat, I made just as many mistakes as I was able to complete tasks properly.

These challenges reminded me of a graduation speech Pema gave for her granddaughter's class, which was turned into the book *Fail, Fail Again, Fail Better*. I found myself failing over and over again during those long, hard months, but I didn't feel like I was getting better at it, as Pema suggests. Janet's final days took every ounce of energy, patience, and compassion I could muster.

I don't know how I would have survived the duration of her illness and death without the on-the-spot practices I have come to rely on. I chose to walk the mile to her skilled nursing facility each morning, as this provided some quiet time for self-reflection. This helped me to maintain a broader perspective. Pausing and taking a few breaths aided me to meet Janet's periodic hallucinations with as much patience and compassion as I could muster. Breathing in the pain and sending out compassion for all of my family and the many others who were going through similar circumstances allowed my heart to remain open through the heartache. I would remind myself that our multidimensional nature allows us to live within paradox and to seek meaning even during some of our most difficult times.

The stress was wearing on me and I lost ground with word finding, memory, mathematics, and my ability to retain information. As the family grieved and recovered after Janet's death, I had hoped these symptoms might improve again, but it appears that these changes have become one more step on my path of neurocognitive decline.

Recently my mother has been diagnosed with dementia, and I am now her agent for health care and finances. This irony of being responsible for my mother's care while she declines with dementia while wrestling with my own cognitive decline is not lost on me. Again, I am doing my best in a less-than-ideal situation. Mom has a difficult time accepting help. I am coaching her and consulting with the staff at the assisted living facility where she lives, trying to create a good environment for her. I can truly empathize with her need to remain in charge of her affairs as long as possible.

I see a bit of myself in her and realize how difficult it must be to finally admit that it is time to allow others to help her dress, bathe, and remind her of the time and to eat. I can imagine myself having similar difficulties in the future. While accepting this new role for her, I breathe in the loss of independence I imagine she is feeling and breathe out a sense of acceptance and comfort to her and all others in similar circumstances.

The irony of being a caregiver when you are challenged by your own health concerns and diminished capacity is not something I face alone. As we age, we are often called upon to care for a spouse, parent, child, or other loved one. My friend, Sid, who you met in the previous chapter, assists his wife who has struggled with a variety of health concerns and has multiple appointments. He told me that between the two of them, they have medical appointments just about every week. Sid said that being a caregiver is a challenge, adding, "Meditation helps keep it real" as he balances both their needs and their changing roles.

I am reminded of Harry and Gabrielle from Gampo Abbey, and so many others I have encountered in hospice and hospital rooms. Being a caregiver is stressful in itself, but with the added complexity of having one's own health issues, the role can be very difficult to manage. Finding additional support for yourself and the person you are caring for can ease the burden somewhat. Like Sid, I have also found that looking for ways to maintain some balance in my life can help sustain my energy and ability to meet my mother's needs.

The situation with my sister was extreme and unexpected. Not all paradox comes with so much shock value. Having a diagnosis of mild cognitive impairment while still functioning in a relatively normal way is paradoxical in itself. Seemingly I can still carry out my responsibilities and activities for day-to-day living and yet some things have changed. As mentioned earlier, I am no longer reliable, especially when relating to time, dates, and mathematics. In the past few months, word retrieval has become more difficult, yet I can write well as long as I have spellcheck and an online thesaurus to fall back on. Frank has told me that I have unknowingly left the stove burners on, yet I can still throw a quick meal together or follow a recipe if I have plenty of time for prep. These contrasting truths are a part of living with a slowly progressing disease.

IDENTITY AND SENSE OF SELF

My identity as a competent caregiver and my sense of confidence in my ability to manage a crisis have had to change through these experiences. I've had to accept that making mistakes and failing are parts of who I am now. This does not negate my capabilities, but these supposed defects and shortcomings are new parts of my multidimensional nature. I know that only through accepting and relaxing with all these parts of myself will I be happy. But this is not always easy.

Having a change in cognition often means a change in the roles you have taken on in life. Sheri, who I introduced in the last chapter, said she really misses her work as a therapist and realized that a lot of her identity was wrapped up in her profession. Our self-worth is often measured by what we do for a living. Recognizing that this is no longer true takes a fair amount of internal adjustment. Finding new ways to fill my days with a sense of meaning and purpose and learning how to plan when my energy and concentration levels are unpredictable on any given day are a few of the new challenges to my changing sense of self.

In our culture that glorifies independence and mobility, losing the ability to drive is often avoided at all costs as people age in our society. This can be a major blow to one's sense of identity and independence. I know several people with MCI or early dementia who have chosen to give up or at least limit their driving. Others had to stop driving when they were unable to pass a driving test.

I gave up driving almost two years ago now. It was a difficult decision, but I knew I could not in good conscience continue. I would not have been able to forgive myself if I had harmed someone by continuing to drive once I knew it was unsafe for me to continue. I still miss the thrill of getting into the car by myself and going for a drive alone. There was a sweet feeling of escape when I drove across the country by myself years ago. I have been lucky, however, to have a group of friends who have scheduled themselves to be a driver for me, rotating each week. This has given me some mobility and has offered me a chance to connect with different friends throughout the month. I didn't know when I made the decision how I would manage without impinging on Frank's independence. Stepping into that uncertainty led to a positive outcome. Not everyone has such a network of support. For many, losing the ability to drive means their world shrinks down and they can become more isolated. This is an area where more community support can make a difference in many people's lives, allowing them a bit more independence and mobility.

Don't-Know Mind

The phrase *Don't-know mind* assists me in resting my mind in openness when I feel like a failure. When I lose my train of thought, when I forget what I was going to do next, and when I am not sure how to meet my mother's growing needs, I like to remember this phrase. It is okay to not know what is next. I remind myself that it is also okay to not know exactly what I am in the middle of doing right now. If I can pause, take a few breaths, and remember "don't-know mind," I can open myself up to the possibility of whatever happens next. Sometimes this means leaving a project undone or not following through, something I never would have considered in the past.

I attended a group retreat recently where the facilitator was leading us in a variety of guided meditations. He would offer different phrases like "don't-know mind" for us to contemplate while we meditated. One phrase he presented that continues to resonate with me is "allow the world to come to you." As someone whose sense of self has focused on helping others, the idea of allowing the world to come to me instead of running toward a situation or trying to fix it changed my perspective.

This is one way I have found to help me relax into the paradoxes and contradictions that pop up all the time. When I can allow all of life—what I like and dislike—to just be, without trying to change it, things aren't so complicated. I wasn't able to remain in that state when Janet was dying, nor would I have expected to. Crises such as a close death put a strain on every fiber of our being. But now, in the calmer waters of my everyday life, I am beginning to take in the lessons learned through all these various experiences. If I can remain open and connected to myself and others in the middle of the messiness life has to offer, then perhaps I can hold the complexities of my multidimensional self and the contradictory nature of the world around me with open loving-kindness.

ANXIETY

Anxiety is an uncomfortable feeling, and yet some level of anxiety is necessary just to move us forward through life. Chögyam Trungpa Rinpoche called this a basic anxiety that propels us toward our desires and propagates our fears. This basic anxiety is its own paradox. We wish to be happy, yet when we gain things that we think will make us happy, we then worry about losing them or we wish for something else. Like the old adages "you can't have your cake and eat it too" and "the grass is always greener on the other side," we tend to want what we don't have and not appreciate what we do have. This level of anxiousness is very familiar once you look for it.

Anxiety has a bad rap. We think of anxiety only in the context of feeling too much of it. In many educational theories, it takes just the right amount of anxiety to learn. Too little and there is no motivation. Too much and the student shuts down. When there is just enough anxiety to stimulate learning, it often feels like excitement, anxiety's close cousin. It is when anxiety tops over the middle ground of being constructive—when we feel overly anxious—that it can rob us of sleep, complicate thought processes and decision-making, and hold us back from activities we enjoy. Increased anxiety is a common issue for people with cognitive decline.

Anytime I am tested, I'm handed a questionnaire about depression and anxiety. It seems like an oxymoron to ask a person with cognitive issues about anxiety. I get caught in the chicken-and-egg analogy: Which comes first, the anxiety that decreases my thinking abilities or my decreased abilities that creates anxiety? Learning how to cope and accept this level of anxiety is a new paradox for me. Speaking to others in my support groups, including conversations with Sid and Sheri, I have discovered that increased anxiety seems to be a universal part of living with cognitive decline. Sheri now describes anxiety as her constant friend since being diagnosed with early dementia.

Recently I felt a new kind of angst during a small group meeting on Zoom. I know the group well, and the meetings had been positive and stimulating for me. Suddenly, without warning, when someone asked me an unexpected question, my mind went blank and I felt overwhelmed with panic. This was unnerving, and I had to excuse myself from the group quickly. I retreated to my bedroom for some quiet time.

Being asked to think on the spot while my mind can't process very quickly anymore put me into that state of panic. As I left the meeting, my body was on autopilot, the fight-or-flight response had taken over and I fled fast. As I lay on my bed, I focused on my breathing, allowing the energy of these strong emotions to wash over and through me. Over and over, with each breath, I breathed in the sense of loss, fear, and confusion into my heart center. Tears flowed, a puzzling mix of sadness and acceptance at the same time. On each outbreath I would send spaciousness to these coexisting feelings in the middle of what appeared to be a meltdown. An hour or so later, Frank and I talked about what had happened and I was able to gain a sense of equilibrium again.

This was yet another humbling experience, another moment of recognizing how my changing cognition was having a greater impact beyond just forgetting a word or two now and then.

When I asked Sid how he works with anxiety, he told me, "Meditation has helped me calm down. It [memory loss] can be frustrating. I remember my father, who was diagnosed with dementia. He would get mad at himself when he couldn't come up with a word or a phrase. I don't do that at all because I'm looking at it more through the lens of meditation. It's just another life process. It's happening and I want to make the best of it." He added, "What I'm working on now is trying to keep calm through meditation and being aware and mindful."

When I asked Sheri how she manages anxiety, she told me of a time this past summer when she developed an unwarranted fear of going to bed. She knew it was irrational, but still, it would often keep her up all night. One night, just by chance, she went out to stand on their back porch. She could hear all the night sounds: a chorus of frogs in a nearby pond, the birds settling in the trees, and the breeze through the branches. Sheri told me, "Just breathing with those sounds calmed me." She started doing this every night, allowing her to go to bed and sleep better.

I am taking a lesson from Sid and Sheri as I consider anxiety as a new companion, another piece of the unpredictable and complex nature of my life with decreasing brain cells. Meditation can be a very useful tool when dealing with heightened anxiety. It can help you to stay in the present moment, allowing worry and distressing thoughts to come and go. Just by focusing on the breath for a few moments can calm both your body and your emotions. It is one resource that can easily be used in any circumstance as we always have our breath readily available.

I have found using the practice of breathing in pain and suffering and breathing out relief for myself and others who are also feeling anxious at this very moment, around the globe, to be calming, but it also brings my small-minded worries into a larger context. Using this meditation technique provides me with an intention and sense of fulfillment similar to the feeling of purpose I enjoyed in my work. I can access this sitting on my couch at home, alone, and find connection and meaning as my heart opens to embrace my changing self and all others who are also sitting at home, facing ambiguity and the unknown.

TONGLEN

The traditional Tibetan Buddhist meditation tonglen is the practice of breathing in pain and suffering and breathing out love and compassion. I was introduced to tonglen thirty years ago when I was very new to Buddhism at a workshop led by Pema. It has been one of the main threads in the fabric of my meditation practice ever since.

Tonglen is frequently called a practice of giving and receiving that rides on the cycle of the breath. The basic instructions are to begin by first opening your heart through remembering something that fills you with awe, such as a beautiful sunset or a loved one's smile. Then, as you breathe in, bring to mind someone who is suffering and imagine breathing in their pain. As you breathe out, imagine you are sending them whatever would be comforting for them: love, compassion, a cozy blanket, and so forth. Use your imagination, as it can be anything that you think will help them. Continue to breathe in the pain and breathe out a sense of relief. Finally, imagine extending this out to all beings who are suffering in similar ways, as much as you can, being sure to include yourself.

You can also practice tonglen for yourself and your own suffering. Begin again with a sense of openness, then breathe in your own pain and breathe out relief and compassion to yourself. Once you have established this cycle, extend the giving and receiving to include all who are suffering in a similar way. This is a way to connect internally with your pain while recognizing that what you are feeling is universally felt by millions of others at the same time. All beings share a desire to be happy and to avoid pain and suffering. When I am able to relate with my pain and relate it with others who are also feeling this same sort of worry or anxiety, I connect on a visceral level with them. Somehow these thoughts and feelings become more bearable.

Some people worry that breathing in others' pain, or even their own, will harm them. I equate this with concern that talking about death and dying will induce death. When you are doing tonglen, you are working with your own breath, imagination, and intention. This may change you, but you cannot catch someone else's disease by this practice. If this worries you, begin with practicing for yourself, then extending it out to others as you are comfortable. Over time, you will find your capacity and confidence in the practice growing.

It is best to begin with small issues rather than jumping into the most severe kinds of suffering. You can then build up your tolerance and meditative muscles. A good starting point is something that is mildly annoying—perhaps the dog that is barking constantly outside your window or the mosquito buzzing around your head.

The intent of tonglen is not to change anything or magically devise a miracle. It is a practice of opening up your heart to the pain, suffering, care, and love that is at the core of our paradoxical lives. At the same time, there are rare instances when your practice may have a positive impact on someone else.

When I was a hospice chaplain, I worked with a young mother who was dying from advanced breast cancer. Her household was lively with relatives coming and going. We had developed a close rapport over several months. On my last visit, I could see that she was entering the phase of actively dying, quietly resting in a liminal state, yet the household was as frenetic as ever around her. She was very weak, barely opening her eyes, and her voice was soft and thready. She asked me to just sit with her for a while. She had her eyes closed while I sat next to her bed, holding her hand and practicing tonglen for her and all others who were dying at that time. After a few minutes, she opened her eyes and said, "I don't know what you are doing but please keep it up." My intention was not to change anything for her, just to sit with her with an open and caring heart, but tonglen clearly was a comfort for her in that moment.

Generally, tonglen is done as a part of a formal meditation at first. To begin tonglen in your formal meditation, I suggest using what I call a tonglen sandwich. Begin with a form of basic meditation for, say, five minutes. Then practice tonglen for ten minutes, and end with another five minutes of basic meditation. This is a lifelong practice that may seem complex and fabricated at first. By beginning in a formal setting, the sequence of the practice can become more natural. Once you are familiar with the process, you can then use tonglen as an on-the-spot meditation whenever it is appropriate. I use tonglen to work with my uncomfortable feelings as well as when I feel helpless witnessing suffering, such as while I watch the news reports about war-torn nations.

~

GUIDED MEDITATION

Formal Meditation Practice of Tonglen

Start with a few minutes of calm-abiding or another basic meditation practice you are familiar with.

First Stage

Pause for a moment and bring to mind an image or feeling of spaciousness, such as a wide-open sky, the ocean, or a sunset—something that inspires a sense of awe for you.

Second Stage

To begin the cycle of giving and receiving, start by imagining you are breathing in completely hot, heavy, thick energy (sense of claustrophobia). Then breathe out cool, light, bright energy (a sense of freshness).

Many of us tend to either breathe in very deeply the pain and barely breathe out relief, or conversely, barely breathe in the pain but send out a big exhalation of calm or peace. The breath in and out should be equal, so that you are not extending one over the other.

This stage only needs to be as long as it takes for you to feel the rhythm and for the energetic exchange and the breathing cycle to be in sync.

Third Stage

Breathe in a specific painful situation, opening to it as fully as possible, then breathe out a form of relief. The topic of the situation can be whatever comes to mind. You can begin with a person or animal you know is suffering, or you can use a part of yourself that is painful.

This is the main portion of the practice, so take your time and allow the thoughts and images to shift as you practice. The intention is to continue to relate to the suffering in whatever form it takes on the inbreath, and relief in whatever form it takes on the outbreath.

Fourth Stage

Extend tonglen further to include all people, animals, and beings who are suffering in a similar way. This can also take some time to develop. You may want to begin with imagining the people in your neighborhood, then those in your town or city, and then begin to extend that to everyone in this country, and then beyond the borders of this country to all we share this planet with. At first you may only get through those in your neighborhood or city. That is a fine starting point and allows you to expand and develop your capacity for imagining more over time.

Ending the Session

To end, let go of the tonglen practice completely and rest your mind through calm-abiding meditation or another basic meditation for a few minutes. Allow your thoughts and feelings to come and go like leaves floating by on a stream.

On-the-Spot Tonglen Practice

For on-the-spot tonglen, you can shorten the first and second stages, mainly focusing on the suffering at hand, such as your own pain when feeling lost or confused, or the suffering of a crying child and their exasperated parent in the grocery store.

Connect with your breath for a few rounds, then begin the sequence of breathing in the situation at hand and breathing out what you imagine would relieve the tension or pain. Do this for a few minutes or a few rounds of breath. Then drop the practice.

8

Allowing Grief and Loss to Flow through the Body

Grief sneaks in
At the breakfast table,
On a foggy morning
With no clear path forward.

An unexpected tear
Slowly warms my cheek.
I realize a loss—overlooked,
As I was too busy to notice,
While trying to hold it all together.
—SHARON LUKERT

As I prepared to write this chapter, I read through an essay I wrote less than two years before. In it I outlined a story of how I companioned a hospice patient with dementia who was grieving the loss of her husband. When I reread it, what struck me the most was the essay included so much more detail than I can recall now. This may seem like an insignificant change at first glance. But with each lost memory or forgotten word, it can feel like a part of myself is drifting away like the evaporation of a dewdrop in the morning sun, almost unnoticed. Small moments of realizing a new loss come often with mild cognitive impairment and early dementia. I try not to dwell on them, as my life is still so full and rich, but I also know not to push these feelings away.

Grieving is a part of life. It is an expression of our connections and the impermanence that pervades all of our world. Most of the time, we can ignore impermanence as our bodies, thoughts and plans, and daily activities can seem so solid and long-lasting. Usually it takes a major shift to shake up our complacency. A tragic loss of a job, house, or loved one brings home the reality that nothing lasts forever. It is a different experience, however, when the loss is slow, chronic, and incremental whether due to poor health, loss of certain capabilities, or any unrelenting form of suffering such as war or famine. Any loss, sudden or recurrent, can feel surreal and unsettling.

UNDERSTANDING GRIEF

Grieving is a natural, active process of adjusting to a loss of any kind. This process involves our thoughts, feelings, physical sensations, and all of our senses—our whole being. Contrary to Western society's expectations, there is no time line for grieving. Through the passage of time, often longer than we can imagine, we can accommodate the new reality of what we have lost, but grieving never really goes away. It can, however, become integrated and woven into the fabric of our lives. Since grief is a natural response to loss, grieving does not need to be feared, suppressed, or embellished. A healthy form of grieving is possible.

We often think of grief as mourning after the death of a loved one. This is one form, but losses occur all the time. There are the minor losses such as losing a pair of eyeglasses or breaking your favorite mug. Disappointing in the moment but not monumental. But if the missing eyeglasses or broken mug are symptoms of cognitive and functional changes, the incident can become a marker of a deeper internal loss of memory or cognitive ability. This can bring up fear and worry about losing more independence and abilities in the future. Those living with mild cognitive impairment and early dementia encounter this form of grief regularly.

In this chapter, I will focus on understanding and coping with the losses that accompany neurodegenerative disease. Bereavement and loss as a part of the dying process is a larger topic than I can fully cover here. There are many books available to support someone after the death of a loved one but few that describe the type of grieving associated with the continual losses experienced with a chronic condition like mild cognitive impairment.

How we experience and cope with loss is unique to each person. Although I have counseled many people through their grief, I can only speak with any authority from my own experience. There are some theories about grieving and coping with loss that can provide a framework for understanding the overall picture of grief. Here I will introduce just a few and share my perspective on the cycle of grief. You may find that taking a larger view of grief can help you navigate your journey through it.

The Cycle of Grief

Elisabeth Kübler-Ross was a pioneer within the death and dying field and, in the 1970s, the first to identify some of the emotional responses a person has during the dying process. Although her linear description of the process was a limited perspective, her theory opened the door to new models for grieving. Many theorists and psychologists have offered their own versions to help us understand what normal grieving looks like.

Lucy Hone is a psychologist and author who went through a devastating loss of her teenage daughter. In her book *Resilient Grieving: How to Find Your Way through a Devastating Loss*, she describes a model for coping with grief in the shape of a jigsaw puzzle. It is made up of various ways she found helpful for her grieving process. She found that no one method for coping was sufficient. Instead, each different expression of grief can be met with a response appropriate for that moment. Kübler-Ross promoted the recognition of the emotional aspect of loss, and Hone provides a variety of tools to work with the grieving process. Both of these models have informed my approach to grieving and coping with loss.

I imagine grief in a cyclic fashion, similar to what we can observe in nature. Grief is a complex repetitive course of loss, adaptation, and resilience circling within us like the earth circling the sun. Like the seasons of the year, grief varies in degrees of intensity and can be unpredictable similar to the weather. During wintertime, we may have inviting white snow and perfect weather for ice skating or the land may be stark and barren. Summer can be filled with warm days, perfect for a growing season, yet a tornado could come sweeping through, leaving a leveled path in its wake.

Just like a tornado can strike down a cornfield in the middle of a warm summer day, grief can catch us off guard when shopping at the grocery store, in the middle of a holiday gathering, or when reading an old essay from a few years ago. Grieving is a labor of love and loss that can be unpredictable and at times messy and overwhelming.

Over time, we as humans have found ways to cope with the seasons and the unpredictability of our climate. We often talk about the weather, prepare for storms or floods, and have on hand the proper gear for when we need it. I see working with loss the same way. If we understand it and feel prepared to deal with it, we can develop a finely lined coat of resilience to comfort us through some of the worst storms of grief.

Grief doesn't happen in a vacuum. Our grieving is often mixed in with our daily lives and obligations. This can be bittersweet, as life goes on somehow while we mourn our losses. This past year I was responsible for preparing the Thanksgiving dinner. The dinner was a success in that it was a time for our small family to gather and include the loss of Janet in our first holiday without her. At the same time, the preparation was really too much for me given my cognitive challenges at this time. I realized this was also the last holiday dinner I would prepare. In this way, the interconnection of the family's need to acknowledge the loss of my sister and my personal loss of a level of functioning wound up together like a tangled ball of yarn. I was glad to be together and sad at the same time.

Anticipatory Grief

When you are faced with a future loss, such as a new diagnosis of a terminal disease like Alzheimer's disease, you can feel sad about the loss of future hopes and dreams. This occurs for all involved: the person with the diagnosis and their family, friends, and loved ones. We often project ourselves into the future as we plan for retirement or write up a bucket list of places to visit and things to do. It can be as ordinary as the desire to watch grandchildren grow up. When these dreams and plans are threatened, we grieve the loss of the future we had hoped for. This is what is meant by anticipatory grief. This kind of loss can be hard to identify and talk about, but it may come up as frustration or resentment toward others, including the medical system or the disease itself. Everyone involved has lost the future they dreamed of, and the changing roles can impose limits that no one expected. It can take time and attention to adapt to this new potential future.

Now, while I care for my mom as she slides into a severe form of dementia, a part of me is also aware that she is showing me what my future may look like some day. This adds an additional layer to my sadness and heartbreak as I also grieve for her.

Chronic Loss

Cognitive decline is an example of amplified impermanence in motion. This disease shatters the illusion of permanence and stability on a daily basis. When I spoke with Sheri about this aspect of the disease process, she asserted that people with cognitive issues become masters in the art of loss because the diminishment of capacities is constant. During my recent neurocognitive test, I was not surprised that my word-finding abilities have decreased, but I was surprised that my ability to learn and retain new information had declined. I value my identity as a lifelong learner, so this new result challenges that self-image; another piece of my identity has changed. Chronic loss can increase anxiety and decrease confidence. Losing abilities incrementally necessitates adapting to a new reality on a regular basis, which is tiring and at times confusing.

How We Experience Grief

In my work as a bereavement counselor and chaplain, I have seen grief take many forms. Often I found my job was to assure the person or family that their responses to grief were okay and appropriate. There is no right or wrong way to feel when grieving. This is also true for the ongoing undercurrent of loss in the lives of those with chronic illness and decreased memory. Each person grieves in a unique way. When a group of people are going through a shared loss, their thoughts, feelings, and needs can vary quite a bit. It can be helpful to keep this in mind because it is hard to know what someone else might be feeling without exploring it with them. For families, this means being open to the differing needs of each person. One may need to be alone, while another may want the comfort of closeness. Being aware of these differing expressions of grief can open our hearts to tolerance and compassion toward one another. Grieving is not static and includes innumerable experiences of thoughts, feelings, physical sensations, and existential questions.

Thoughts and Emotions

One may feel a plethora of emotions: numbness, confusion, denial, anger, irritability, frustration, curiosity, depression, regret, relief, or sadness. All of these and more are normal emotional responses to loss. To me, the only issue is if a particular emotion becomes solid and stuck for a long period of time. Emotions are meant to be fluid and shifting, as we've discussed earlier.

I often feel sadness as a first reaction to one of my "Oh no" moments of forgetfulness. But there are times when denial follows quickly after. Denial gets a bad rap and is often considered a form of avoidance. I see denial as a normal, necessary, and helpful part of grief and acceptance of difficult situations. Our body and psyche can only take in so much change at a time. I think of the flow of denial, in and out of consciousness, as a way that our psyche adjusts slowly to a radical shift in our reality. As long as denial doesn't become a conscious and fixed refusal to accept the circumstances, it can be a sort of psychological relief valve in difficult times.

It has been surprising to me lately to notice the small, unconscious ways denial can show up. Sometimes—especially on a good day, when I feel energetic and perfectly capable of functioning—I think there was a mistake and I've been misdiagnosed. It can be hard to believe that there is really anything wrong. Of course, the bad brain days are harsh reminders that chase away any sense of denial. I can catch myself daydreaming about driving somewhere when suddenly I remember that I don't drive anymore. Often my heart sinks a bit when I remember the truth. Then I take a few breaths, feel that heartbreak, breathe out, and carry on.

All of these emotions may color our thoughts and increase distraction. Our emotions and thoughts are so intertwined that it can be difficult to really pull them apart. If I am focused on a new symptom, I can become obsessive about it: "What does this mean? Are things progressing or is this new issue a typical part of aging?" Obsession can lead to increased fear and anxiety. I try not to stay in a state of obsession too long while also allowing myself some time to consider these questions. It becomes a matter of balance, to not push these thoughts away or try to stop them, which is impossible anyhow. At the same time, I try to not dwell on the obsessions either.

My dreams have also shifted. There are times I am more confused and disoriented in my dreams than during waking hours. I was surprised when this started to happen. I believe this is one way my psyche is adjusting to a possible future with severe dementia on a very subtle level. When I first took monastic vows in 1997, I had a similar experience. I was suddenly in monastic robes in my dreams and would remember the vows I had taken as a guide to my actions within the dream. Our dream life can help us make peace with our changing daytime reality.

Grief Resides in the Body

We hold our emotions in our bodies. This is one of the gifts of being embodied, and we can often access our feelings by paying attention to our physical sensations.

In 2000 I tended to a family as their loved one died in the intensive care unit. A few weeks later, the wife contacted me for a consultation. She had been having pain in her chest, which her physician assured her was not a heart attack. As we talked, she realized that she had been trying to "get over" her grief, but her heart was truly broken. It was a relief for her to hear that this type of response, physically and emotionally, is not uncommon. Knowing this helped her move into a more active phase with her grieving, and allowed the sensations and emotions she experienced to ebb and flow.

In the perpetual grief of a chronic illness, the physical sensations may be small and recurrent. I mentioned the sensation of my heart sinking. This is an actual feeling, not a metaphor. Loss is often felt in the trunk of the body, at its core. Lungs might feel tight, the heart can hurt, and the gut can feel twisted in knots or nauseous. All of these can be physical expressions of grief. Tightened muscles, tapping fingers, and deep sighs can also be expressions of grief, anxiety, confusion, or resignation. Everyone's body has a language of its own. It's a matter of learning to listen.

We can learn a lot about our emotions if we listen to what our body is telling us. If I am feeling particularly anxious, I can stop and take a quick scan of my body: "Where am I feeling tense? Is there additional heat or coolness somewhere? Am I nauseous or hungry?" I don't try to change anything as much as listen to what might be behind these sensations. Maybe I'm really hungry, or maybe anxiety is playing a role in my growling belly. I have asked myself what sadness tastes like: "Is it sweet or sour? Does it have a smell?" The answer doesn't matter as much as the act of paying attention using all of our senses.

Often we seek physical comfort when grieving. A warm blanket, a hot bath, exercise, or a walk in the woods—all these are ways for soothing grief physically. I have a long-standing relationship with music, so I can get in touch with my emotions through the sounds of an orchestra or a simple melody. Moving to music can foster this connection even more for me. Whether I am interacting with a painful or joyful feeling, music and movement are ways for me to relate to and express my feelings. You may have another way to get in touch with your grief through the interconnection of body, mind, and spirit. Whatever method works for you can be a doorway toward integrating the grieving process and discovering resilience and strength within it.

COPING WITH LOSS

Human beings are built to cope and adapt. Most of us have gone through some sort of loss in our lives and have survived, perhaps even grown and thrived because of these tough times. Many of you reading this have developed your own way of coping and have developed some resilience as a result of your previous experiences of loss and grief. A healthy attitude toward and embracing impermanence can become part of blending change and loss into our sense of self. This is how we build resilience emotionally and spiritually. This, in turn, can support a happier and more fulfilling quality of life. This resilience can support us as cognition changes, when many forms of loss are inevitable. We can learn to accommodate and accept these changes with a little grace.

Coping Strategies and Tools

You may already have your own tried-and-true methods for coping with grief. In this section I will provide a brief outline of a few of the tools I rely on to work with grief and loss. You may find one or more of these appeal to you, or this outline may inspire your imagination to discover other ways to welcome grief when it is knocking at your door.

LEANING IN AND LETTING GO

Often our first reaction to change is to resist. I have learned to allow this first impulse to bloom fully and then to pay attention to what I feel and do next. Pema Chödrön often speaks about leaning into the hard spots. I think of an analogy of having a sore calf muscle. If I begin to massage it, moving deeper into the sore spot, the muscle can relax and let go of the spasm or knot of tension. In the case of working with loss, we lean in emotionally and physically to feel deeply and allow the feelings and sensations to relax. If we continue to resist, the tension can build up until the emotion feels like a tornado ready to sweep through us.

Leaning into our grief doesn't always feel good. Leaning into loss can feel overwhelming and intensely sad. Right now I am struggling to care for my mother and work with her caregivers to provide for her as her needs are quickly changing. I am also dealing with my sadness around losing my mom and struggling to keep up with all of this while dealing with my own cognitive decline.

Last week I was completely overwhelmed, unable to sleep or stop obsessing about her care. My grief was all tangled up with the practical issues that needed to be addressed. I tried taking a hot bath, going for a walk in the woods, and journaling, but nothing could cut through the obsessive thinking and deep sadness I felt. It wasn't until one morning while listening to some quiet music and washing the dishes that the tears began to fall. These turned into sobs. It felt like I could cry forever. After a while, they subsided. I washed my face and decided to call on some additional support to help me cope with the situation. I needed to lean in and allow myself to feel the depth of this loss and worry about my mom, compounded with concern for my ability to meet her needs. Sobbing over the dishes did not feel good in the moment, but it did allow me to move forward with more clarity and a fresh perspective.

I don't always understand what I need or how to let go when I am in the midst of a loss. For me, it takes trust to follow my intuition and allow my body to express my feelings. This is a subtle internal mode of working with grief. The letting go that can occur can't be forced.

Rather, letting go is a natural response to leaning in. Leaning in can be gentler than the sobbing session I described above. Often our feelings come up quietly and repeat over and over again. Then the leaning in happens in "a touch-and-go fashion" as Chogyam Trunpga used to say. Like the Pause Practice, allowing the feelings to rest in your heart and then letting them dissolve. These responses to loss tend to visit us in a cyclic pattern. Leaning in can allow these thoughts, feelings, and sensations to come and go, and this can give us the time we need to adjust.

Learning to lean in and let go is embedded in the disease process of cognitive decline. Sometimes the letting go is involuntary, as memories are lost, but there is also a healthy form of letting go when one can relax with the changes. I am reminded of Sid's earlier description of relaxing with forgetting and accepting losing his words as just another part of life.

DOES THIS HELP OR HARM?

In her book *Resilient Grieving: How to Find Your Way through a Devastating Loss*, Lucy Hone discussed the roller-coaster ride of her grief and an approach she had developed to avoid wallowing in despair while also allowing herself the space to feel all of her emotions. She would ask herself the question, "Is this helping or harming?"[14] Simple and direct.

I've begun to ask myself, "Is this helpful or harmful?" as a way to avoid falling down the rabbit hole of obsessive, anxious thoughts. When I was first diagnosed, I lost a lot of sleep because I would spend hours at night searching the internet for information. Hours of midnight Google searches only fed my fear and worry. These were not helpful. But a well-informed search for specific information about a particular symptom or treatment assists my medical decisions and is helpful. Now when this urge to surf the web one more time comes up, I ask myself, "Is this going to help or hurt?" Often just asking the question calms the anxiety-driven itch to open my computer and look, one more time, for some intangible truth.

JOURNALING AND ARTWORK

In earlier chapters, I mentioned writing in a journal as a way to develop self-reflection. It can also be a means for working with ongoing loss and grief. If I am having a particularly difficult day, I may only write one word—SAD. Just naming it, allowing the sadness to exist on a piece of paper, loosens its grip on me and I can let go a little and relax with the feeling. Once the sadness is proclaimed, I can breathe with it, allow it to reside in my heart, and look with curiosity at why it might be visiting me on this particular day. Other times, I just doodle. Scribbling can release a lot of tension as I don't even have to try to make sense out of it. The scratchy, jumbled-up lines can be a preverbal expression of something I can't capture in words.

If you have artistic inclinations, you may find engaging in your artwork to be a refreshing outlet for expressing your grief. Even if your abilities in writing, drawing, painting, playing music, and the like are less than they were earlier in your life, the point here is for personal expression, not to create a beautiful work of art.

SUPPORT

Talking with others about your feelings can support a healthy way to cope with the ongoing challenge of loss due to changing cognition. Whether you find friends, a loved one, a support group, or a therapist to be helpful for you is a matter of personal preference and your particular circumstances. I have found that there are certain things that are easier to share with a group of peers or a therapist than with a loved one. I am aware that Frank is adjusting to my changing abilities, and I often don't want to burden him further. I believe that having other outlets to express my feelings, such as my support group and therapist, is a way to keep our relationship strong while maintaining some autonomy between us.

TIME IN NATURE

Forest bathing, a new fad, describes what many have known for centuries. Time in nature is healing. Being out in nature is soothing to our nervous systems and can slow down our speedy minds. Some studies have shown that as little as fifteen minutes outdoors can have a positive impact on your mood and body. Whether I am out hiking on the bluffs, kayaking on the Mississippi, or sitting in my backyard watching the birds, I feel energized and refreshed from feeling the warmth of the sun on my face.

If you have limited access to the greater outdoors, you can still benefit from sitting on your porch or near a warm, sunny window. Watching a video of the ocean or a beautiful landscape can have a similar effect on your body, mind, and spirit.

FINDING HUMOR IN DAILY LIFE

Finding humor in my daily life allows me to loosen up and not get too bogged down in the stickiness of grief. Of course there is sadness, but not all of grieving is gloom and doom. There are moments of levity as well. These moments can help us keep our equilibrium and not take ourselves or our condition so seriously all the time.

Frank and I have developed a playful way of noting a change in my skills. This helps me to maintain high spirits as my cognition shifts. Early on, I asked Frank to help me recognize cognitive changes, as I realized I may not be aware of some shifts. He was hesitant at first, but as he realized that I appreciated the feedback instead of getting defensive, this became a more playful interaction for us. He began keeping a notebook and writing down his observations, which we review together from time to time.

Now, there are occasions when he will comment in the moment. If I am searching for a common word or forgetting something we had just talked about, he will point it out to me on the spot. He will playfully call out in a sing-song voice, "There's another ding." This light-hearted approach makes us both laugh. He is calling me out as if I just pulled the "go to jail" card during a game of Monopoly rather than as a judgmental critique. Maybe it's a loss, but it's no big deal. I have found that humor and grieving can be close companions. When blended together, they have the capacity to open our hearts with warmth toward our losses and our blessings.

FAITH, HOPE, AND FINDING PURPOSE

One of the biggest lessons I learned when working in hospice was the power and flexibility of hope and faith. As a person's situation would change through the dying process, what they hoped for would change too. One patient I remember started out saying he hoped he wouldn't lose his ability to walk. When he lost that ability, he then hoped he could continue to wash and care for himself. When he needed to let go and allow others to help him, his hope turned toward a peaceful death.

What we hope for gives us a sense of meaning and purpose. This is beyond any particular religious belief or doctrine. This is a basic human capacity to imagine ourselves in the future. What we hope for is personal and changeable. How we express this hope may be shaped by our faith or existential beliefs. Prayer is often an expression of our hopes and fear and our faith and beliefs.

Finding a sense of purpose is an empowering way to integrate loss and grief into our lives. Sheri has used her tough experience with the medical system to educate medical and therapy students. I have used this new sense of purpose to write this book. Others may find purpose by maintaining connections with family members or their faith group, being out in nature, or through travel. Whatever nourishes your faith, hope, and sense of purpose can be a strong balm for the ongoing impact of grief.

SENSING GRIEF IN THE BODY

We have already talked about how tuning in with your body can be a way of connecting with grief and encourage adaptation and resilience. This can be done simply by paying attention to the sensations in your body. The next time you feel tense or uncomfortable, take a moment to become aware of that physical feeling. If you stay with the sensation for a few minutes and ask with curiosity what is associated with that tension, you may discover some thoughts and feelings you had not been aware of.

Exercise is a great way to move emotion that may be held within the body. Like being out in nature, exercise can be stimulating and refreshing. It can also be a way of releasing any pent-up feelings you may have. As the body moves, so do our thoughts and emotions.

Receiving a massage can release tension in the body and any emotions that may be held in our flesh and bones. It is not unusual for someone to become tearful for no conscious reason while having their shoulders massaged. As the muscles relax, emotions you had not been aware of may come bubbling up to the surface. You can feel calmer and lighter after a relaxing massage.

The body scan meditation is a contemplative practice that can also foster this connection of the body, mind, and spirit by allowing you to relax into the tensions and any pain in the body. This is another way to release any emotions that may be held in the muscular tissue. I have found that practicing a body scan can help me relax with my sadness, anxiety, or worry. It is easiest to perform a body scan with a guided meditation. You can find these online or in most meditation apps.

Each of these strategies for coping with grief, as well as any others that you have discovered on your own, can be applied when they feel appropriate or necessary. Just as the grieving process is fluid and changing, so too are our ways of coping with loss. One day I may need to have a hard cry. On another day, a long walk near the river allows me to integrate the ever-present grief while remembering that loss also holds within it love, compassion, and connection.

~

GUIDED MEDITATION

Body Scan

There are several forms of body scan meditation. Quite a few of these can be found on YouTube. I will relay the basic sequence for a body scan meditation, but it is easier to practice this form of meditation when it is guided. In the resources section at the back of this book, I have provided a small sampling of the body scan meditations that are available on YouTube at this time.

A body scan can start at the top of your head and work down to your feet, or it can begin with your toes and work up toward the crown of your head. It is a matter of preference. You may find that one feels more natural to you than the other.

Begin in a comfortable position, either lying down or sitting in a relaxed but upright posture.

Take a few slow, deep breaths and feel the rise and fall of your chest as your lungs expand and contract. Bring your awareness into your body, allowing any outer distractions to fall into the background.

Now bring your awareness to your feet. Imagine that you are breathing into your feet. You may want to wiggle your toes, point and flex your feet, and then allow them to relax.

What sensations do you feel here? Is there any area that hurts, that feels tight, hot, or cold? Just allow these sensations to be. With each area of your body, repeat this exploration. Go through the different areas of your body at a slow pace, allowing a few rounds of breath with each.

Next, repeat this as you bring your awareness to your legs, first breathing into your calves, tightening and relaxing them, and then into your knees and thighs.

Move your awareness and breathe up into your pelvis and buttocks, and your lower back.

Now bring your breath and awareness to your middle torso, front and back. Pay attention to how your belly feels, and allow your belly and back to relax.

As your awareness moves into your chest and upper back, again pay attention to any pain, soreness, tension, and areas that feel hot or cold, and breathe slowly and deeply into these areas.

Bring your breath and attention to your shoulders, moving slowly with the breath down each arm, down to your fingers. You can open and close your hands a few times to help them relax.

Moving up to your neck, gently place your attention to this area where we often hold tension. Breathe in and out, noticing any sensations you may have here.

Bring your awareness up the back of your head and slowly wrap around to your ears, mouth, cheeks, eyes, and forehead. Allow your jaw to rest in a slack position, releasing any tension around your mouth. Continue to bring your awareness up to the top of your head.

Once you have completed this cycle, you can remain for as long as you like. You can relax your attention, breathing naturally, and rest in this calm and restorative state of mind.

9

Facing the Unknown with Openness and Curiosity

Strength is a soft, agile, and open mind that bears witness to life, rather than trying to fight against or live around undesirable experiences. Strength is our willingness to stay present in the face of uncertainty.

—ELIZABETH MATTIS NAMGYEL, *The Power of an Open Question: The Buddha's Path to Freedom*

While contemplating the words of the Buddhist teacher Elizabeth Mattis Namgyel, I am reminded of Anna, the hospice patient introduced in chapter 1. She taught me such an important lesson about facing uncertainty with a gentle and open mind. Staying present when thinking about a future with declining cognition and the possibility of severe dementia in the future is not a simple task, yet it is possible.

Life, even without this particular challenge, is not easy to face at times. Often we do not get what we want, or if we do, we worry about losing it and then mourn the loss when things change. I can't say that I have ever wanted to develop Alzheimer's, but it seems to be what life has presented me with. So now the question becomes: How do I deal with the uncertainty of the future with a bit of openness, including the grief, fear, and worry that are natural responses to this situation?

One thing is certain: even when there is a terminal diagnosis, no one knows how they will age or die or what the end of life will be like. I tend to think of end-stage dementia as my most likely cause of death as I am fairly healthy otherwise, but I could be hit by a bus tomorrow or develop pancreatic cancer long before the neurodegenerative disease becomes fatal.

When I think about my future health and quality of life, I try to use my imagination to think about the multiple possibilities ahead with curiosity. This isn't a quick one-and-done sort of process. I tend to mull over different potential outcomes over a long period of time. It's like having a variety of different seeds in my hand and tossing them out into the garden. Over time, some of the scattered seeds will begin to take root, others will never sprout. Only a few will survive and thrive as a mature plant. The future is a kaleidoscope of possibilities for everyone. Thinking about it in a playful way can open the door to considering the future with some levity and flexibility.

So how can one prepare for the unknowable future? Mattis Namgyel suggests developing a soft and open form of strength, which seems like a good place to start. In *The Power of an Open Question: The Buddha's Path to Freedom*, she points to the power of an open question. This is a form of contemplation I use when thinking about the future, whether regarding my plans for a trip this summer or the end of my life. The act of considering our future health with openness to a variety

of possibilities goes against our social and cultural norms. It takes brav-
ery and strength to do so. So here I am asking you to step slowly and
gently into topics that are ignored or forbidden in many families and
social circles. Using the approach of an open question can allow the exploration of things that remain unknowable to unfold at a natural pace,
without forcing the issue or neglecting any insight or clarity that may
arise about your unanswerable questions and uncertain future.

OPEN QUESTIONS

When contemplating an open question, the goal is not to find the
answer but to see where the question leads you. In Buddhism and
contemplative Christian practices, holding a question that can't
be answered is a form of meditative practice. Zen Buddhism calls
such questions koans. An open question or a seemingly nonsensical
statement—often the case in a Zen koan—can stimulate curiosity
even if the question appears unsolvable. It is something to chew on
over time. Something that piques your curiosity and tugs at your
heart. A question to live by. These sorts of questions can haunt you,
in a positive way, bringing into focus what is most meaningful to
you and inviting vitality into your life. They can energize your imagination, inspiring poetry, song, and creativity.

During my early journey into the new territory of Alzheimer's
disease, inquiries into what is the meaning of life and illness and what
happens after death became foremost in my mind. I asked my long-
time teachers for their thoughts. I pondered these esoteric and unanswerable questions throughout my days, during meditation, and into
my dream life. I can't say that I've found a universal answer to these

age-old questions. However, I did find a growing sense of calm and resolve. It was as if by holding these questions they became familiar friends rather than negative omens of future pain and suffering.

Since I am still floating in the headwaters of my personal path with cognitive decline, many ongoing open questions remain. Often this type of inquiry takes on a life of its own, popping up unexpectantly and evolving over time. I try to allow them to glide in and out of my thoughts with a light touch and some curiosity as to where they may lead.

Recently I was feeling stressed as my mother's needs were changing faster than I could keep up with. I found myself overly anxious and frustrated with her caregivers, who were also trying to adjust. One morning as I was meditating, I realized that I needed to bring more gentleness into the whole situation. I wasn't sure what that would look like, but I began to set an intention of being gentle at the start of each day. The thought of gentleness carried over into my conversations with my mom, allowing me to be more patient with her increased confusion and repetitiveness. I began to understand her caregivers' points of view and personal struggles to keep up with my mother's ever-changing needs.

One morning, after a series of phone calls with social workers, the doctor's office, and the care facility, I sat on the couch with a headache brewing. It seemed like my mother's care had become so complex, and I was receiving conflicting advice. Then the word *gentleness* popped into my mind. Now I needed to apply this to myself. I unplugged the phone and took a soothing hot bath to relax my mind and body, slowly adjusting emotionally to this new situation and added responsibility.

My inquiry into how I can be gentle with myself and my mom, and how to bring gentleness into the whole situation of her care, continues to reverberate throughout my interactions. Gentleness calms my shredded nerves and assists me to work with these challenges with a bit more flexibility and openness. This type of inquiry was also beneficial when Frank and I first began to confront the many logistical implications of my diagnosis as well.

FUTURE EXPECTATIONS

Death and dying, along with chronic illness, including dementia, are systematically ignored in our society. Our culture is oriented toward healthy youthfulness. Imagine all the industries that would go out of business otherwise. Social avoidance of these basic facts of life makes it more difficult for Alzheimer's disease research to find funding, devalues private and professional caregivers, and silences many conversations about the unavoidable truth that someday, and in some unknown way, we will all face illness and death. I saw this daily in my work as a chaplain.

Most of us have a mental image of what our future and even our death will look like. Often this is based on previous experiences or family histories. Finding out that Alzheimer's disease or a related dementia is a likely part of your future can change that image and what you think is possible. However, even with a terminal diagnosis, the future remains uncertain. Although there is a social taboo against thinking about death and dying, it can actually be liberating to do so. Contemplating your death is another practice found in Buddhism and other contemplative traditions. It is often said that by thinking about our own death, we can live a fuller and richer life. Contemplating death and dying has been a part of my Buddhist meditation for years.

In order for a chaplain to truly be present for someone facing the end of life, they must have already reflected on their own thoughts, beliefs, hopes, and fears about illness and death. To this end, I have taught a personal death awareness course to students for many years. Most chaplain residents have had extensive training within their faith tradition, but few have considered their personal attitudes toward death and dying.

In my course, I used an experiential exercise that guided the students through six different death scenarios. These hypothetical deaths varied from a sudden death due to a car accident to dying from Alzheimer's disease in a skilled nursing facility. I would prompt the students to notice what thoughts and feelings came up and how each scenario would impact their priorities differently, now and at the time of death. This would lead to a deep and often emotional group discussion.

Inquiring into your own thoughts and feelings about death and dying may seem scary at first. But if you hold the topic with a light touch, like a dream or an open question, you may be surprised at what you discover about yourself. Each time I consider my death, I learn something new about my attitude toward life, relationships, and current priorities. This can be a way to touch into what your spiritual and emotional needs are now and what they may be in the future. Being aware of your feelings, beliefs, and priorities can help guide you through planning for both your spiritual and practical needs for the unknown future.

LOGISTICS AND PLANNING

I am a lifelong planner, and considering future needs is one of my coping mechanisms. Yet I can't ignore the emotional difficulty when thinking about future changes and the potential loss of my independence. Before having any meaningful discussion about future care needs, I found it necessary to first work with the hope and fear that accompany such discussions. What am I afraid of and why? What do I hope for? What can be addressed now, and what will remain unknown? These can be important open inquiries to allow for a full consideration of all possibilities with as much clarity and openness as possible.

Since finding out I have mild cognitive impairment, I have heard it said that one of the benefits of an early diagnosis is the ability to plan for the future. This is true, though it can seem like a daunting task. At the same time, it is important to me to plan for the future while I am still able to fully participate. There are so many practical concerns to address such as finances, health-care decisions, future housing, and caregiving needs, to name a few.

It can be difficult to take all of these issues on at once. Fortunately there are avenues for support and advice. Contacting your local Area Agency on Aging is a good first step. Each state has a designated agency, though they may have another name. In Wisconsin it is called the Aging and Disability Resource Center (ADRC). You can also check your local chapter of the Alzheimer's Association for classes and information.

PROBLEM-SOLVING MODEL

There are many ways to approach an issue, but when it seems as though there are a number to focus on all at once, it can be overwhelming. This is even more true with mild cognitive impairment, as problem-solving can be mentally challenging. Frank and I found Healthy Living with

Mild Cognitive Impairment, a local course through the Wisconsin chapter of the Alzheimer's Association, to be educational and support-ive. One of the classes introduced us to a problem-solving strategy that we have used to map out a time line to address the astounding number of legal and financial issues one at a time. It has been helpful to break down the topics into more manageable pieces in this way.

Frank and I knew we needed to begin working with the logistical issues posed by my changing cognition, but we weren't sure where to start. We decided to use the problem-solving strategy to sort things out. We sat at our kitchen table overlooking the yellow cup flowers surrounded by buzzing bees and dragonflies outside our window. Frank with a cup of coffee, I with my tea, we were both equipped with yellow legal pads, pens, and heads full of worry.

The process begins with identifying the topic or problem and then brainstorming every aspect of the issue you can think of. We chose the topic of future planning. Brainstorming is a way to allow yourself to think about every possible angle regarding an issue with-out judging or dismissing anything that comes to mind. That comes later, but with brainstorming, the idea is to write down as much as you can. Once the problem or topic is well flushed out and written down, then you begin to brainstorm about possible solutions, record-ing your ideas in another column or on a different page. We wrote down a few pages of future-planning issues, concerns, and questions, then we listed possible actions needed to address each one, until we couldn't think of any more.

We ended up with a very complete but lengthy list of things to do. The next step in this model is to decide what course of action is best for you from the lists you have made. We decided to sort out what issues needed immediate attention, what could wait a while, and what was either the lowest priority or would remain unknown for now. These became our three lists: the "A list" for immediate needs, "B list" to address in a few months, and the "C list" to address later. In reality, it took us close to a year to complete the A list, and we are still working slowly through the B list, while the C list has become more of a contemplation for the future. We keep these lists on the front of our refrigerator as a constant reminder of what we can do to prepare for the future. We have also come to accept that this process of preparation can take a lot of time and thought, and that we need to approach these topics that can seem so serious and consequential with patience, flexibility, and humor.

Using this type of problem-solving may not appeal to you, but finding some way to talk about these issues can be so beneficial for both the person with the illness and their care partner. It takes an emotional toll to worry about future logistics. Keeping silent about your concerns can be isolating and could cause unnecessary distance and misunderstanding. Sometimes a facilitator such as a counselor or pastor, or a webinar like the one we attended, can begin to open up these deeper conversations. In my experience, facing these issues brings some sense of relief, while avoiding them can create fear and anxiety for everyone involved.

One logistical element I feel compelled to promote is the need for a well-thought-out advance health care directive. Professionally, I was an advocate for advance health care planning. As a chaplain, I witnessed the distress of many family members who did not know what their loved one's wishes were in an emergency or for end-of-life care. Given this past experience, having a detailed power of attorney for health care in place and holding honest and detailed conversations with those who were likely to be my decision-makers in the future were major priorities for me. This was one of the first logistical tasks I undertook to be sure my loved ones were familiar with my wishes. I revised my previous document as my preferences had changed, so it now reflects the possibility of a long, drawn-out process into the end stages of dementia while also addressing my wishes if I were to have a sudden, unexpected health crisis. We can't predict the specifics of what may occur, but providing some sense of what makes life worth living and some of your medical preferences can help your family and medical team make difficult decisions at a time when you are unable to speak for yourself. Whether I die in two weeks or twenty years, my loved ones will know what my wishes are. This is a future gift we can each provide for our loved ones.

PLANNING FOR YOUR EMOTIONAL AND SPIRITUAL FUTURE

We are such complex beings, not one part can fully define us. Even when a person may not be able to respond in a familiar way, that does not mean that the person doesn't have something to say or share with us. The emotional and spiritual need for connection continues throughout our lives, including into the hazy period of severe dementia. We are relational beings. It is through relationships that we express our emotions and experience our spirituality. Whether we are relating to a deeper part of ourselves, to another person, with nature, or with God, those relationships don't end with dementia. But the relationships do change.

My mother reminded me of our multidimensionality. She lives in a world that is confusing and, in her words, "all scrambled up," yet she is still smart and witty at times. Although she struggles to know if it is day or night, she knew that I was writing a book and often asked me how it was going. Mom found comfort in the things she has known best throughout her life: sports, music, and her nursing career. We continue to do our best to help her maintain these areas of interest, though her attention is waning. She still loves to share stories about her earlier years working as a young nurse in labor and delivery. We may have heard these stories hundreds of times, but for her, each telling is like capturing a part of who she is that she can still hold on to. Her emotional need at this time is to remain as connected as possible with her own interests and identity, and her family and friends.

Laurayne, my mother-in-law, lived her final years with dementia in a skilled nursing facility. Although her words became inaudible, more like stutters and mumbled syllables, she still loved her visits from family. She seemed confused about who was who, but that didn't seem to matter anymore. Laurayne would sometimes become frustrated as she tried to tell us something. The family would lean forward and try to understand what she was trying to convey. Often she wasn't able to say it, but the respect the family showed her in continuing to try to understand expressed their love to her. She basked in this love, smiling and giving hugs, in spite of the frustration of trying to communicate. She was a role model of how I hope to continue to try to reach out to my loved ones, even if my words are gone and I may not recognize them anymore.

Someone who has been involved with prayer and ritual may find these to still be meaningful, just as the woman I visited who teared up when hearing Psalm 23. I have seen those who have been nonverbal for a long time join in reciting the Lord's Prayer when praying out loud with them at their bedside. I hope to have some of the Buddhist mantras and songs that I love recorded so they can be played for me whenever I am no longer able to recite them myself.

You may want to ask yourself, "How might I prepare for my spiritual needs in the future?" It could be choosing photos of significant places and events to be hung in your room; listening to uplifting music, a favorite television show, or a movie that makes you laugh and helps you to relax; favorite prayers or a verse you know well and find comforting. These can be included in your written plans for the future. This planning is for all parts of who you are. You may find some creative and personal ways to nurture your emotional and spiritual well-being in the future.

Humane Caregiving for the Later Stages of Dementia

In our society, recent generations do not enjoy the same kind of community support that was common in earlier times. In the United States, a family often feels very much on their own when facing caregiving at home, in a care facility, or from a distance for their loved one. The United States is also confronting a health-care crisis, including an exponential number of people who need care for Alzheimer's disease and related dementias. I wrote earlier about the stigma attached to this disease. I believe that if this stigma were lessened, there would be more compassionate, affordable, and diverse care options for people as they enter into the end stage of the disease. This would lead to less fear and trepidation throughout the course of this illness.

Recently there has been more research regarding best practices for caring for a person living with severe dementia, and many care models have been developed to meet this need. However, our health-care system is vast and disparate, so it will take a long time for these models to become standard practice. Knowing a little about the basic elements of these models can help inform your search for care for a loved one or while planning for your own eventual needs.

Most of the care models are based on person-centered care, which means the health care is integrated with the individual's goals, values, and preferences. How this is implemented can vary from one model to another, depending on the setting. Care coordination, including an ongoing care plan, and psychosocial interventions are other aspects of most dementia care models. Finding one that is near you, affordable, and accessible can take a lot of research on your part. Again, finding the support of local nonprofit agencies, such as the Area Agency on Aging, can help ease the exploration for support, whether you are looking for in-home or facility care.

There are several books on the market about communicating with and supporting those with Alzheimer's disease and other related dementias. *The Complete Family Guide to Dementia: Everything You Need to Know to Help Your Parent and Yourself*, by Thomas F. Harrison and Brent P. Forester, MD, came highly recommended to me. I am using this book as a companion as I navigate the fresh waters of my mother's decline. I have learned to shift away from vague questions, as this is now too difficult for her to think through quickly and respond. This one simple tip has improved our nightly phone calls as I no longer ask how her day was, which usually just led to a long, deep sigh on her end of the phone. As a person likely to experience further cognitive decline in the future, this is a book I will recommend to my family.

I am learning quickly that caring for my mother's needs is a constantly moving target, as her abilities and needs seem to be changing quickly. I am so grateful for the support of her caregivers and her doctor, who have been very involved in trying to find the best and kindest way to care for her. My hope is that the models for person-centered care will become the standard of care across the many levels of service, from home care, assisted living facilities, and skilled nursing facilities, and within the clinic and hospital settings. Until the health-care system becomes fully educated about and a friendly environment for people living with dementia, the system itself can at times be an obstacle to optimal care.

How we can best engage with the system comes back to asking some basic questions about what is most important to you at any given moment, and how we can be as prepared as possible for the unknown future given the current state of the health-care system.

UNKNOWN POTENTIAL

All of the logistics and future planning mentioned above are important parts of preparing for the unknown future, but the essence of what I want to convey is the beauty, love, and mystery that is so vital and always possible for living our best life, at any stage. It is easy to forget that on a very personal level, this sort of faith and magic can exist in every moment.

Magic and Mystery

Chewing on these big questions about life and death, I can't ignore the magic and mystery that can happen, even in the most ordinary moments. There are the daily flashes of magic when seeing the first robin returning for spring, shared laughter with a friend, and the warmth of a smile from a passerby. These moments and many more can be cultivated within the realm of severe dementia with some effort and intention. The magic may be fleeting and quickly forgotten, but these moments can be cherished for what they are—a brief respite from confusion and disorientation for the person and a memory to cherish for the family and caregivers.

I have seen times of magic when a woman who, unaware of her surroundings, still lights up when hearing a familiar voice. A man who can no longer feed himself can play the keyboard when guided to the piano. These precious, intimate moments have proven to me that we don't lose our basic nature and that magic can still happen even while living with dementia. This does not negate the struggles of behavioral issues, possible psychosis, and other challenges that progressive dementia presents. But it can remind us that through respect and trying to understand the emotional and spiritual needs of the person, there is still room for this magic to happen.

Betty* lived in a skilled nursing facility that I visited regularly as a hospice chaplain. She was in a constant comatose state, with no visible response to me, her thin arms lying limp at her side. Our visits were very one-sided. Her room was usually quiet and dim, with few personal effects visible. Often I would stand at her bedside and hold her hand, speaking to her about the weather or an upcoming holiday, wondering how she was, and wishing her well. I had this type of visit with her monthly over the course of a year. It had become quite routine, and I became accustomed to her nonresponsiveness.

Then one day when I visited, she had a greeting card pinned to her bulletin board. I decided to read it to her, including the signatures of the people who sent it. Suddenly she opened her eyes and had a big smile. She said, "Wasn't that lovely of them to send that!" I was stunned. I replied in amazement, "Betty, so nice to see you! How are you?" She responded, looking at me with a sparkle in her eye, "I'm wonderful." She paused, "A man came and sang to me, and this made me so happy." And then, just as quickly, she was silent, her eyes closed, and there was no outward sign of consciousness again.

I was taken aback by this encounter and shared this with the hospice team at our next meeting. Her nurse, Bob, stood up and said, "I sang to Betty the week before your visit." We were all awestruck. This woman that everyone thought was unaware of her surroundings was moved by Bob's song. She was also moved enough by the card her dear friends had sent to bring her up into consciousness, just for a brief time. To witness her visible pleasure and peacefulness was one more sign of the magic and mystery that is possible in every moment of our lives. I hope we can all stay open to the songs that touch us, the music that moves us, and the loved ones who embrace us, no matter what state our body and mind may be in.

ENGAGING WITH AN OPEN QUESTION

Asking open questions can be a passage into understanding your deepest wants and needs and setting priorities for today and the future. It can allow further clarity about your values and beliefs, which can guide your choices. It is not unusual to face deep esoteric questions when dealing with a neurocognitive disease. This diagnosis challenges how we think about ourselves and what constitutes our identity. By holding these difficult questions with gentleness and patience, the questions themselves become a part of the journey.

A question is a way of engaging your imagination and curiosity. When we access our creativity, there is the potential to be surprised by what we discover about ourselves and the world around us. I take heart in this form of open inquiry. It is like a great experiment as I never know exactly where the question will take me.

This sort of inquiry requires patience and curiosity. I invite you into this pool of patience with me, as we immerse ourselves in the unknown mysteries and deep questions that shape our lives at a deep and subtle level. Within the most sorrowful tale there lies a hint of a potential promise—a promise of hope for a future that is not as bleak and not as black and white as most of us assume. There are nuances of gray and gold throughout the experience of Alzheimer's disease and related dementias, from the first moments of realizing something is wrong, up through the final days and hours of someone's life. I wonder what questions each of you may have and where they may lead you at this time in your life.

GUIDED MEDITATION

Contemplation of an Open Question

To begin a contemplation of an open question, it can be helpful to have a particular subject or question in mind. This might be very vague at first. It can help to write it down in your journal or on a sticky note close by, where you can occasionally be reminded. Your question can be as deep as the meaning of life or as ordinary and whimsical as "Why is the sky blue?" The purpose is to engage your imagination and see what naturally arises. Once you become familiar with this way of holding a question, you may discover new inquiries you had not considered before. Honoring these types of questions can become a kind of guide or signpost as you meet change in every way that it may arrive at your door in the coming years.

There is no right or wrong way to work with an open question. If you have a meditation practice, you may want to try holding a question in mind during a practice session. If you enjoy journaling, then writing about the question may be your means of exploration. I often find that the questions come and go, as I mentioned before, and can come up at any time. It seems when I am out in nature or gardening in my backyard, my mind is at ease and more open to expanding beyond my typical way of thinking. When my body is busy with exercise is another time that I find new ideas can pop up without my trying to track them down. Discovering how you relate to open questions is an adventure of its own, with no special equipment or training necessary.

Here I am providing a short list of questions as a way to help you begin this process. You can use these as a jumping-off point and see where they lead you on your personal journey. These questions may be simple for you to answer or they may become your own koans, so to speak. You may have other burning questions that touch you deeply. Whatever avenue you pursue, I hope your journey with these inquiries opens up new, unexplored territory and a deeper understanding of your true nature.

When do you feel loved and when do you feel loving toward
others?

What do you look forward to, and what do you fear in the
future?

If you imagine your death, what does it look like and what do
you want to be sure others know?

How can you invite more gentleness into your life?

What is most important for you now?

What brings you joy and wonderment?

Epilogue

As I near the end of this book, I am grateful for the opportunity for self-reflection and exploration. When I started journaling about my interactions with my dementia ancestors, I had no idea where it would lead. I am thankful for the journey they have taken me on. This book is as much to honor them as it is for you, the reader. I hope our exploration together has opened your heart to the many opportunities for love, care, and understanding that are possible for everyone affected by cognitive decline, no matter its cause.

But the end of a book is not an end to the story. Each one of you, like me, will continue to experience what it means to age. Whether you are someone with cognitive issues or a caregiver—or you find yourself in any other type of dynamic and shifting circumstances— change is inevitable. If one or more of the stories and tools shared in this book helps you and eases your journey just a little, then my aspiration has been fulfilled.

There is one more story from my work in hospice that I have not yet shared. The book feels incomplete without including the insight from this one patient I came to cherish. I'll call her Frances.

On my last visit with Frances*, I didn't know it would be my last. She was sleepy, half-reclining in her new bed in a skilled nursing facility, legs crossed, and deeply snoring when I arrived. She was so happy to see me as she woke up. Through drooping lids and slurring words she asked me to stay, even though she was having difficulty staying awake.

We slowly talked about her new room at the nursing facility where she was admitted just days before. She said she was settling in, surrounded by her tchotchkes, books, and photos. "But you know, I still get depressed," she said, slumping back in the bed. We whispered about acceptance and courage. I told her I saw both in her. We shared a poem by Mary Oliver, one of her favorites.

Then she perked up for a moment, intent on sharing her thoughts. It was a struggle as the new drugs made her drowsy. She fought to get the words out and would drift away midsentence. But as she reawakened, still searching for the right words, she shared a newfound understanding. Word by word, in between dozing off, her insight emerged. She made me repeat it back to her verbatim. She spoke of her apartment, a place where she had found peace and solace after years of homelessness. She had to leave that sanctuary the week before as her condition worsened and necessitated round-the-clock care.

"It's like God sees you as so special he gives you a gift so precious that even if it lasts just a moment, you know you are loved. Like holding a well-cut jewel made of ice. As you hold it, it melts, but it is so beautiful, you can't put it down. But the tighter you hold it, the faster it disappears. You have to just let it be an incredible jewel of ice and love it for what it is while you have it. It makes the gift that much more poignant and vivid, knowing you can't hold it for very long."

Once Frances was satisfied I understood her, we said goodbye, hoping to see each other again soon. I promised to write down what she said and bring her words back to her, but that moment proved to be another icy jewel that I couldn't hold on to. She died soon after this visit. I have held on to Frances's gift for more than twenty years. Although I didn't have the chance to read her words to her, I am grateful to be able to share them with you now.

This book has been an icy jewel for me—the writing of it a gift, keeping my mind strong and clear for now, until my memory fails. And now I need to let this jewel go as I pass it on to you. Now the book is yours. I hope that you will find your own jewels of inner strength, curiosity, and perhaps even joy to buoy you through all the emotional and spiritual challenges that may lie ahead.

Resources

BOOKS

Anderson, Nicole D., Kelly J. Murphy, and Angela K. Troyer. *Living with Mild Cognitive Impairment: A Guide to Maximizing Brain Health and Reducing Risk of Dementia.* Oxford: Oxford University Press, 2012.

Bolte Taylor, Jill. *My Stroke of Insight: A Brain Scientist's Personal Journey.* New York: Plume, 2009.

Chödrön, Pema. *Fail, Fail Again, Fail Better.* Boulder, CO: Sounds True, 2015.

———. *How to Meditate: A Practical Guide to Making Friends with Your Mind.* Boulder, CO: Sounds True, 2013.

———. *How We Live Is How We Die.* Boulder, CO: Shambhala Publications, 2022.

———. *Taking the Leap: Freeing Ourselves from Old Habits and Fears.* Boulder, CO: Shambhala Publications, 2019.

———. *When Things Fall Apart: Heart Advice for Difficult Times.* 20th ann. ed. Boulder, CO: Shambhala Publications, 2016.

———. *The Wisdom of No Escape: And the Path of Loving-Kindness.* Boulder, CO: Shambhala Publication, 2018.

Hanh, Thich Nhat. *The Art of Living: Peace and Freedom in the Here and Now.* New York: HarperOne, 2017.

Harrison, Thomas F., and Brent P. Forester. *The Complete Family Guide to Dementia: Everything You Need to Know to Help Your Parent and Yourself.* New York: Guilford Press, 2022.

Hone, Lucy. *Resilient Grieving: How to Find Your Way through a Devastating Loss.* New York: The Experiment, 2017.

Mattis Namgyel, Elizabeth. *The Power of an Open Question: The Buddha's Path to Freedom.* Boston: Shambhala Publications, 2011.

WEBSITES AND ORGANIZATIONS

Alzheimer's Association

https://www.alz.org

The mission of the Alzheimer's Association is to lead the way to end Alzheimer's and all other dementia—by accelerating global research, driving risk reduction and early detection, and maximizing quality care and support.

Area Agencies on Aging

https://www.usaging.org/adrcs

Each county has an Area Agency on Aging to offer local support, resources, and education regarding a multitude of issues such as housing, caregiver support, volunteering, and other activities. Many have a dementia specialist who can assist a person living with cognitive changes and their loved ones access specific programs and resources. If you put in a google search for the Agency on Aging for your state, you will find a website that can direct you to your local agency.

Atlas of Emotions

atlasofemotions.org
Developed in collaboration between the Dalai Lama and the psychologist Paul Ekman, Atlas of Emotions is a wonderful interactive site that breaks down the mechanism of emotions and physiological responses.

Coping with Loss

https://www.copingwithloss.co
Dr. Lucy Hone and Dr. Denise Quinlan apply their research and training in positive psychology to help people understand and cope with grief.

Dementia Matters Podcast

https://www.adrc.wisc.edu/dementia-matters
Dementia Matters is an educational podcast series about Alzheimer's disease and other causes of dementia, offering helpful information and current trends in research, diagnosis, and treatments.

Share the Care

sharethecare.org
Share the Care is a nonprofit organization that offers a guidebook and tools to provide support for caregivers using a model to assist people in organizing supportive care groups.

INSTRUCTIONAL VIDEOS FOR MEDITATION PRACTICES

"9-Minute Body Scan: Anxiety Skills #31." Therapy in a Nutshell. June 27, 2019. YouTube, 9:12, https://www.youtube.com/watch?v=6IA TiVQ1u58.

"The Body Scan: A Beginner's Mindfulness Meditation." Sharp Healthcare. July 2, 2019. YouTube, 7:31, https://www.youtube.com /watch?v=kH-OQn5Ui8g.

"Body Scan Exercise, Jon Kabat-Zinn." Be You Fully. January 26, 2017. YouTube, 29:02, https://www.youtube.com/watch?v=15q-N-_kkrU&list=PLqgKqZJtDXE4LY8tarf VX5lae3TqM-8gE&index=2.

Chödrön, Pema, and Oprah Winfrey. "The Exercise That Could End Your Suffering." Oprah Winfrey Network. October 19, 2014. YouTube, 3:07, https://www.youtube.com/watch?v=L9r_X6aX6HA &t=1s.

"Mindfulness Exercise: Body Scan." Policy Research Associates. January 13, 2022. YouTube, 6:24, https://www.youtube.com/watch?v=e0f-9wa2SUX0.

Tsoknyi Rinpoche. "Beauitful Monsters and Handshake Practice." Pundarika UK. March 30, 2017. YouTube, 15:57, https://www .youtube.com/watch?v=LgB64s3itv8.

Notes

1. "Mild Cognitive Impairment," Alzheimer's Association, accessed April 6, 2024, https://www.alz.org/alzheimers-dementia/what -is-dementia/related_conditions/mild-cognitive-impairment.

2. Alzheimer's Association, "Special Report—More Than Normal Aging: Understanding Mild Cognitive Impairment," 2022 Alzheimer's Disease Facts and Figures, https://alz.org/media/Docu ments/alzheimers-facts-and-figures-special-report-2022.pdf.

3. Pema Khandro Rinpoche, "Breaking Open in the Bardo," *Buddhadharma: The Practitioner's Quarterly Magazine*, January 2, 2022.

4. Ani is a prefix signifying someone is a Tibetan Buddhist nun.

5. Luke 17:21.

6. Dzigar Kongtrul, "Becoming a Bodhisattva in Modern Times," Mahayana Seminar, Talk 3, Mangala Shri Bhuti, Vershire, VT, 2009.

7. Hyun Duk Yang et al., "History of Alzheimer's Disease," *Dementia and Neurocognitive Disorders* 15, no. 4 (2016): 115–21.

8. Jesse F. Ballenger, "History of Medicine, Framing Confusion: Dementia, Society, and History," *AMA Journal of Ethics* 19, no. 7 (July 2017): 715.

9. Jesse F. Ballenger, "History of Medicine, Framing Confusion: Dementia, Society, and History," *AMA Journal of Ethics* 19, no. 7 (July 2017): 715.

10. Jesse F. Ballenger, "History of Medicine, Framing Confusion: Dementia, Society, and History," *AMA Journal of Ethics* 19, no. 7 (July 2017): 717.

11. "Alzheimer's Association," Alzheimer's Disease International, accessed June 26, 2024, https://www.alzint.org/member/alzheimers -association/#:~:text=The%20Alzheimer%27s%20Association %20was%20founded,advance%20research%20into%20the%20 disease.

12. Pema Chödrön, *When Things Fall Apart: Heart Advice for Difficult Times*, 1st ed. (Boulder, CO: Shambhala Publications, 2000), 16.

13. Madhukar Dwivedi et al., "Effects of Meditation on Structural Changes of the Brain in Patients with Mild Cognitive Impairment or Alzheimer's Disease Dementia," *Frontiers in Human Neuroscience* 15 (2021), https://doi.org/10.3389/fnhum.2021.728993.

14. Lucy Hone, *Resilient Grieving: How to Find Your Way through a Devastating Loss* (New York: The Experiment, 2024), 20.